WHY
can't you
catch me
BEING?
GOOD?

To Victer, Teena
& the three girls

Love,

Eydie Denken

26 Principles of Raising Self-Confident, Well-Behaved Children

WHY can't you catch me BEING GOOD?

Edythe Denkin, Ph.D.

Adams Media Corporation
Holbrook, Massachusetts

Published by
Adams Media Corporation
260 Center Street, Holbrook, MA 02343. U.S.A.
www.adamsmedia.com

ISBN: 1-58062-273-9

Printed in Canada.

J I H G F E D C B

Library of Congress Cataloging-in-Publication Data
Denkin, Edythe.
Why can't you catch me being good? : 26 principles of raising self-confident,
well-behaved children / Edythe Denkin.
p.   cm.
ISBN 1-58062-273-9
1. Child rearing. 2. Parenting. 3. Parent and child. 4. Child psychology.
5. Parents—Psychology. I. Title.
HQ769.D433 2000
649'.1—dc21   00-023819

This publication is designed to provide accurate and authoritative information
with regard to the subject matter covered. It is sold with the understanding that
the publisher is not engaged in rendering legal, accounting, or other professional
advice. If legal advice or other expert assistance is required, the services of a com-
petent professional person should be sought.
— From a *Declaration of Principles* jointly adopted by a Committee of the
American Bar Association and a Committee of Publishers and Associations

Cover photo by Stockbyte.

This book is available at quantity discounts for bulk purchases.
For information, call 1-800-872-5627.

~

Dedication

To Allan E. Sloane, my teacher and mentor whose mind and spirit are woven within the fabric of this book. I couldn't have written it without you. To my husband, Eddie, for his continued support in all of my endeavors, and to each of my boys for their confidence in me, and to their wives-to-be so they may have the pleasure of enjoying parenthood as much as I did.

To my cousins Edie and Rodney Robb, and my friend and advisor, Ginny Pangallo, whose help was invaluable. To Sheila Pakula, who painstakingly edited for me, to my secretary, Willie Gentry, Marola and Lenny Goldenberg, my Aunt Claire Glider, and my nephew Mitchell Rosenberg whose encouragement was always there— thank you. And to each of my clients, whom I have taught, and who, in turn, have taught me what they and their children most need today—and how to help them find it.

And, of course, to you too, so that you may find your own happiness, and you may raise calm, and confident children. Enjoy the moments, for they pass all too quickly.

~Table of Contents~

Part One:
Rules for Growing Self-Confidence—
Principles I–IX

Part Three:
Discipline Is from the Inside—
Principles XX–XXVI

Foreword

Most of us are constantly being told what we do that is wrong, not what we do that is right. No wonder unhappiness is rampant. I notice it wherever I go. Yesterday, when I played golf, one of the foursome criticized himself mercilessly. When his long shot went either too far to the left or to the right, he berated himself, "That was stupid. What's wrong with you? Don't you ever get it right?" When he had a 175-yard ball down the middle of the fairway (that was good for his ability), he said nothing, and behaved as if he should have played that way all along. He wasn't a pro, yet he couldn't give himself a break. Yesterday wasn't unusual at the golf course. It happens almost every time I am there. I see many people denigrating themselves or their children continuously.

One day as I was hitting golf balls at Arnold Palmer's Golf Course in Florida, I overheard someone say, "That was a great shot, Arnold." I looked up, and it was Arnold Palmer. I watched him practicing, and was astounded at what I saw. He hit a wedge shot 100 yards, and shouted, "Yes!" applauding his accomplishment. I've made this kind of shot many times and never complimented myself for it. But Arnold Palmer did! He did the same thing at the putting green. When he hit a short putt, he complimented himself. So Arnold Palmer focused on what he did right, and practiced it over and over again. I saw a winning

XII WHY CAN'T YOU CATCH ME BEING GOOD?

formula in play that day. You can have it too. Could that be one ingredient that helped make Arnold Palmer a pro?

This book is about you, and how you perceive what happens to you. It is about the fact that you react to your children in the same way your parents reacted to you, and how you can change that. Becoming consciously aware of when this happens can make a difference in your life, and in your family. You can begin to raise yourself and your children with positive regard, and create unstoppable people. Each week practice applying one of the principles given in this book by constantly focusing on what each of you is doing right. Love, acceptance, and approval are needed to build confidence and self-assurance. Remember to follow through on what you say and to never give up. Take one step at a time. Finally, convince your family, and yourself, that mistakes are your teachers; you can learn from them. Then you too will have a winning formula.

The Chinese say, "A trip of a thousand miles begins with the first step." When you are encouraged—in your first steps—by focusing on what you do right, your confidence grows. Your journey becomes easier, more fulfilling. Working through your worst frustrations often brings a breakthrough. Instead of berating yourself with what you should have done and didn't, adopt the attitude that things happen as they're supposed to. Relax, and learn from your mistakes. They happen for a reason and are supposed to help you grow.

This book is about the reason mistakes occur, and how you can react differently by focusing on what you and your children are doing right, letting go of criticism, and finding positive ways to learn and correct seemingly impossible situations. In the process you will build happiness, self-esteem, and develop confidence in your ability to make a difference in your life and your family's life.

❧ Introduction ❧

When I was raising my boys I didn't know that I would learn about who I was from the way I parented them. It was quite a journey, and it changed me. In the beginning I was a perfectionist, and as critical of my children as my parents had been of me. They loved me, and I loved my children, but a deeper part of me knew I wanted to raise my children in a more positive way. For most of us, childhood is difficult and painful, even though as adults we remember little of it. Yet it is that foundation that drives our unconscious behavior and makes us who we are.

I found parenting to be a mixture of fun, worry, and insecurity. It was wonderful when we went to the beach, built huge forts in the sand, and rushed to make the walls high enough to withstand the incoming tide. In those moments I became a kid again. I relived much of the fun and the fears I had had during my childhood.

Each of our boys, at about age five, asked me to marry him. My heart melted. The question was easy to answer because I had read about how to handle it. I explained that I couldn't marry them because I was already married to their father. My worry and insecurity came from the other questions and situations that I knew nothing about. I didn't want to harm my sons by saying the wrong thing. I remembered what hurt me when I was little, and

I loved my boys so much that I felt overwhelmed by the enormity of the job. What if I didn't get it right?

I wanted to make my children's world perfect. I didn't realize that they also would try to be perfect—like me. At the time, I wasn't aware that children absorb the feelings of their parents, and subconsciously live by them. Perfect is an enormous task for little people. If I had it to do over, I would tell them, "There is no such thing as perfect. Mistakes are our teachers, and we learn from them." That would have made a difference. It would have helped my children and me to relax about who we were. We would have understood that it wasn't necessary to be perfect.

This book contains twenty-six principles that I've developed through thirty-one years of parenting, fourteen years of teaching, and seventeen years of being a therapist. I believe these principles provide the basic foundation of confidence. They are structured to give you the security to know you are doing what is right for yourself and your children. I have included illustrations of each principle, and how they can be applied to your life. When you realize how simple and effective these principles are, I hope you will be able to relax and have fun while raising your children, and redoing your own childhood in the process. Although times will change, the principles won't. I hope to guide you to be the best you can be, to know that that's quite enough, and to enjoy each day.

~ **Chapter 1** ~

Our Perceptions

How Our Perceptions Affect Us

It's not what happens to us that is important. It is our response that makes the difference. One person can experience tragedy and perceive it as the universe teaching him a great lesson. He may feel that if he heeds that lesson, and find value from it, the course of his life will change. Another person can experience a similar tragedy, and see it as a sign that no matter what she does, life will never turn out right. She is meant to have pain, and there's nothing she can do about it.

Many successful men and women have come from lives of great tragedy. But their persistence and positive outlook precluded them from wallowing in self-pity. Instead they chose to use their early childhood experiences as a challenge to understand what happened and why; and what they needed to do to ensure they would not repeat their parents' failures.

The way we approach life begins with our perceptions: how we perceive what happened to us, our acknowledgment of its effect on us, and most important, our decision to react differently from this day forward. Our perceptions will affect our attitudes. If we are willing to look at the role our perceptions play, and then adjust our attitudes, we can make great strides.

In parenting, we must consider not only how our children react to us but also how we perceive their reactions. If we

1

perceive their behavior as a means of purposely hurting us, our reactions are quite different than if we perceive their behavior as merely a way of getting their needs met.

Our perception of each child differs according to the genetic predispositions that the child brings into the world. We react differently to each child because each child acts differently toward us. Our reactions to our children give them a perception of who they are, and how much they are loved and valued.

Wouldn't it be helpful to understand why we react the way we do to our child's actions? Was it the child's mannerism, tone of voice, or choice of words? What unconscious memories did he or she evoke? What happened to us when we were children and acted and reacted the same way toward our parents? Who does our child remind us of?

How Our Perceptions Affect Our Children

When we perceive our children as either loving and kind, or hostile and aggressive, they see themselves through our eyes and behave accordingly. Young children who are forming an impression of who and what they are in this world take their cues from their parents, and what they perceive the children to be.

We are the adults. As parents, we do not need to take their behavior personally. It is what it is! They are doing what they know, and cannot yet be held accountable for what they *do not know*.

We can either take responsibility for the emotional environment we bring to our children, or we can blame their genetic predisposition and choice of friends. It certainly is far easier to place blame than to assume responsibility for our reactions to our children and for the effect it may have on their self-perception.

Since we choose friends who have similar perceptions and attitudes, doesn't it follow that our children will also choose friends like themselves? Therefore, if our children feel as if they are worthwhile, responsible, and well liked, imagine what their friends will believe about themselves? Let's take a look at what may happen if our children grow up feeling like rebels in their own home, never quite getting it right. When children always get "into trouble" for little things (i.e., not cleaning their room, not doing homework, not listening), and rarely are rewarded for what they do right, what will their perception of themselves be? What kind of friends will they bring into their lives when they become teenagers and are free to choose what they want?

Almost every home has one "perfect child" who behaves exactly the way the parents expect. He receives the highest grades and honors, and does everything to win parental approval. But usually there are other children in the same family who do not behave accordingly. They may be rebellious, quiet, funny, the family scapegoat, the victim, or completely aloof. These children may see the unfairness of their parents' response to the perfect child and feel indignant. They may believe that they, too, deserve respect. Some children give up, some give in, and others fight for their rights. The jails are full of those who perceive themselves as "victims." They see their family, and their society, as bad, and behave accordingly. Chances are, they saw themselves as bad while growing up in their family and in school.

If We Can't Adjust Our Perceptions, How Can We Expect It of Our Children?

Can parents have an influence on children who perceive the world as a bad place? Of course they can, unless the parents have that same perception. Their children may be unduly influenced by the parents' negative perspectives, and take it a step further by acting out against the world.

When our children become teenagers they move toward friends who have the same attitudes and perceptions they have. Don't you think the emotional environment we provided for them had something to do with their choice of friends? And that same emotional environment can be different for each of our children, depending on our response to them.

Do you want your children to fear you and their world, and find a way to rebel against it. Or, do you want them to think creatively and express their own feelings? If they are treated as special beings with a unique place in the world, wouldn't that put them on a positive path? Imagine how it would feel to sit back and enjoy watching your children as adults. The alternative might be to find yourself constantly worrying about the problems they always seem to get themselves into. Are you either avoiding them, mopping up after them, or getting them out of trouble? Even a murderer's parents feel distraught about what their child has done. They may blame society for their child's problems, but somewhere they wonder how it might have been if their child's home environment had been different. This path requires adjusting your own patterns, perceptions, and attitudes to effect meaningful results. And what could be more important?

Can we help our children change their patterns and perceptions? Yes, but only if we first change ours. When we are able to hear our children's feelings, to communicate those feelings back to them, and then to adopt new attitudes toward what they have said, they will want to share and learn from us.

Our children also learn by observing what we do to ourselves, not just by what we do to them. Changing our attitudes and perceptions can have a powerful effect on our children, if we really say what we mean and mean what we say. Many people who grew up in impoverished environments, but had loving, supportive, and nurturing parents turned out to be highly respected citizens. As reported in the October 1998 issue of *Time* magazine, successful students from all environments listed their secrets of success as "family support, can-do spirit, persistence, church involvement, and diligence." They all stated that family support made the difference in their lives.

Chapter 2

How to Put Yourself in Control

Parenting isn't about your child, it's about you when you were a child. Stop blaming—it doesn't work. Instead, think about why you lose control, and how you can get it back. Be in charge of your feelings; nobody else is.

Right now you are unconsciously reacting to your child in much the same way your parents reacted to you. You can stop by becoming aware of when these feelings come from your childhood, from the way your parents and other authority figures reacted to you. Your childhood feelings are interfering with the relationship you are establishing with your child today.

You can change all of this by learning how to step out of your circumstances whenever you begin to feel angry. *Stop, look, and be aware!* Acknowledge that you are angry—it's okay. You're only human, but you are not entitled to thrust that anger onto your child.

When I was raising our youngest son, and had finally become aware of many of my feelings, I chose to teach him about his feelings. I was able to teach him differently than I had our older sons, because I was more aware and had more life experience. Watching parents learn becomes a real advantage for children.

One day when Robby came home from school, I met him with, "Robby, I am really angry at you." He was about seven years old, and he stopped me in the middle of my sentence.

"Mom, you're not angry at me. You must have had a bad day. That's why you're angry." "No, Rob," I replied, "I had a good day. I'm angry because you didn't keep your promise to me." He continued, "Mom, that's not why you're angry. What happened to you today?" I told him that I was really feeling angry right then because he wasn't listening to me. He persisted, "Come on, Mom, tell me what happened?"

I began to laugh, and thought, "How could a seven-year-old child have enough perspective to step out of his circumstances and look at mine?" His comments made me stop and think. Then I said, "Well, there were some things that happened to me today that made me feel angry. Then I came home and saw that you didn't put your toys away as you promised. And I really felt angry." We both laughed. Then he said, "Okay, Mom, I'll put my toys away now."

We had communicated in a very special way. We understood and accepted each other. When we talked about him keeping his promises, it was with mutual respect. He did a better job of following through after that, but he wasn't perfect. He was still a child. Again and again he made mistakes, and that was okay. We learn from our mistakes.

At first, it wasn't easy to separate my anger toward my children from the way my parents responded to me. And it wasn't easy to look at my perceptions and assumptions, rather than to blame my children. My older children didn't have it as easy, but they started me on my path. They were active, intelligent twin boys—a constant challenge. When they were just three years old, they came to me and said, "Mommy, we don't want you to yell at us anymore." Surprised, I answered, "But what am I to do when you don't listen?" They said, "Just talk to us, Mommy, we'll listen." Then I asked them what I should do if I talked to them, and they still didn't listen. They made a suggestion, I responded, and together we made a plan. We established boundaries, and consequences, and I followed through on what I said. Before I became a parent, I taught elementary school, and that experience showed me that following through on what I said was more important than anything else I could have done.

• • •

IMPACT in Action

IMPACT is a formula I have developed to help you put yourself in control in order to bring yourself the love and happiness you deserve.

I stands for I.
It means "I have feelings."

M stands for My.
It means "My feelings count." Ask yourself, "What am I feeling now?"

P stands for Perception.
Ask yourself, "What am I perceiving about what just happened?"

A stands for Assumption and Attitude.
Ask yourself, "What is the assumption I am now making? How does it impact my attitude, block my feelings, and change my form of communication?"

C stands for Communication.
Ask yourself, "How can I step out of these circumstances and communicate my feelings about what just happened?"

T stands for Trust.
You are now ready to communicate in a way that will bring understanding and acceptance. Trust that it will work!

IMPACT is an effective tool that will help you stop yourself from saying and doing what you never meant to say and do. It can become part of you, and help you change the patterns you were brought up with. You need to step out of your circumstances and discover why you are reacting in a particular way. In order to understand what is happening when you are ready to explode, take a break. *Stop.* Look over the situation, and the answers will come. After you have uncovered the patterns that were the core of your upbringing, you can become the parent you planned to be.

Your parents didn't mean to wound you. They did the best they could at the time. They reacted to you as their parents had reacted to them. Mostly your parents loved you, but they just didn't know another way to raise you. But now it's time to stop the cycle. You can begin to change the patterns now.

• • •

You Can Do It Differently

YOUR FEELINGS PREVENT POSITIVE COMMUNICATION

Your feelings may also keep you in your childhood, continually getting in the way of raising your children the way you originally envisioned. Instead your children repeatedly arouse old feelings that block you from being who you hoped and planned to be.

Congratulations! When you become aware of your "true" feelings, perceptions, and assumptions, you take your first step toward a new way of relating to your child. Suppose you and Johnny are involved in the usual commonplace provocation. If you truly understand how you feel and what needs to be said, you are no longer enslaved by your old patterns of reacting to familial situations. It can happen. It did for me, and it changed my life in the process. I no longer need to react with uncontrolled anger. I have found a more peaceful way of being. You too can acquire this gift—for yourself and your children!

I know you're thinking, "If I knew why I was losing my patience, I wouldn't have let it happen." Perhaps the following story will illustrate my point.

YOU SEE BUT YOU DON'T SEE

Early one morning while looking at the beauty of Long Island Sound from my bedroom window, I saw several splendid green parrots fly by. It was an astonishing sight, because we all know parrots do not live on the East Coast. I rapped my husband on the shoulder, shouting, "Eddie, wake up, the most incredible green parrots just flew by!" He thought he was dreaming. By the time he woke up, of course they had already passed. We sat there for a while discussing it, but I thought that he didn't believe a word I said.

Later, a friend confirmed my story. Apparently the parrots were being transported from the Andes in South America. At the airport, their crate had been dropped, and they escaped. But they stayed in the area.

Several weeks later my husband spotted them in the evergreen trees along our walk. It was quite a sight. I didn't see them again for a long time. We could still hear their chirping, but we couldn't find them. Recently, when I passed those evergreens, my neighbor asked if I could see the parrots. I couldn't, but I did hear them. She pointed them out, and finally I saw them. Then she told me a book had been written about the episode.

Doesn't life have its paradoxes? There are times when we have to be shown what is there, before we can see it. I would like to help you see yourselves and your children in a very different way. Why don't you sit down, relax, and follow my lead?

A VISUALIZATION EXERCISE

Find a place where you can be alone, and allow yourself fifteen minutes of complete quiet with no interruptions (the bathroom usually works). This can become a place where you can literally step out of your circumstances.

When you feel ready, breathe in deeply to the count of five. Fill your stomach with air, and hold it until the count of five again. Then release the air, while counting backward from five to one. Do this five times or until you are thoroughly relaxed.

Now, visualize one of your children. See, sense, and feel the emotions you have when your child is talking to you in a certain tone of voice or acting in a particular way, or when you are most upset. Do not rush. Continue to relax, step back in time before your child was born, before you were an adult. Be yourself at age five. Observe an event from your past that you still remember. Who hurt you, who shamed you, who yelled at you or treated you badly? Reenact that time.

Try to feel those emotions again. What was it like for you? What person do you remember most? For example, if that person was your mother, talk to her: "Mom, I was only five years old. I couldn't have done anything bad enough to warrant so much anger. Was I acting like someone from your childhood who was mean to you? I didn't deserve to be treated like that. Neither did you or anyone else. What happened to you when you were a child? What could I have done to remind you of a very bad time in your life? I'm sorry you had a childhood filled with anger and hostility, but why did you lash out at me? I didn't deserve it, Mom."

Now think about your child, and ask yourself, "Who is my child reminding me of? Is it you, Mom? What do I feel when my child acts up or acts out? What happens that reminds me of someone from my childhood? Who does my child represent: my good self, my bad self, my mother, father, sister, brother, grand-parents, aunt, uncle? Is it someone from my present: my husband, ex-husband, wife, ex-wife, in-law? My child is not this person. I will work on separating what is happening today from the feelings of my past. My child doesn't deserve my anger. I will find another way to correct her. I can learn to focus on what she does right, not on what she does wrong, and that can change the way I react to her."

Next, ask yourself, "What do I automatically assume? Do I believe she is purposely trying to make me angry? What did Mom assume about me? Did she say I was purposely out to get her, to make her life miserable, or that I was selfish?" Was that really true? Of course it wasn't, but after your mother treated you that way over and over again, you may have wanted to get back at her. Or, you may have felt it was in your best interest to protect your-self. No one else was protecting you sufficiently on an emotional level. But you did not start out that way. All you really wanted was your mother's love and care. You never planned to hurt her or be selfish or spoiled. You were just reacting, the only way you knew how, to the way you were being treated. Nobody had taught you how to react differently. If your mother assumed you were bad, or that you were purposely trying to "get" her, she may have convinced you as well.

I want to help you see that it simply wasn't true. You did not start out bad. You reacted to the way you were being treated, and to the messages you were given. If a child is told he is bad enough times, he will begin to behave as if he were bad.

Now you can change that assumption. Take time and allow yourself to fully realize what the assumption was. What did they always tell you about yourself? Did they say you were selfish or spoiled, or did they treat you as if you were perfect? Maybe none of it was true. You were not bad, but you weren't perfect either. You *were* purposely trying to get love and approval. And you were doing the best you could do, at the time, to get what you needed.

But you were only a child, and you may not have known the right way to get what you wanted. Were you taught what you could do right, instead of being told what you did wrong?

Now step back into where you are right now. See, sense, and feel your child as a child who is asking for what she wants, but not the way you would like her to ask. Think of how you can give your child a better way to get what she wants. Take your time before you react, and allow the answer to come.

REALIZE THAT YOU ARE RELIVING YOUR CHILDHOOD

Allow yourself to recognize that you are also reliving your childhood while you raise your child. For example, think of a special food that you enjoyed as a child. When it is served to you today, notice the memories that are aroused as you enjoy the food. What if you hated liver as a child, and were forced to eat it? How do you feel today when you are served liver? Don't you experience a powerful reaction? What your child does or does not do brings back memories. If your father berated you when you got the fishing line tangled, you may hate fishing today. But if fishing was the only time he spent with you, and he was relaxed and happy, you may look forward to fishing expeditions.

What do you feel when your child doesn't listen to you, or speaks to you in a fresh tone of voice? What is your reaction? What happened to you when you were fresh to your parents, or didn't listen? Or were you the kind of child who wouldn't dare speak back to your parents for fear of what would happen? Does all of this affect the way you react to your child today? Of course it does.

If you have a child who really doesn't do anything wrong, you may have been one of the lucky people who had parents who respected and loved you for who you were. You may have happy memories from your childhood, and you probably don't overreact to what your child does. But what if you have lots of unhappy memories? Suppose you had an alcoholic parent who was depressed, nervous, or anxious most of the time? If so, you lived with the feeling that there was something wrong with you, or that whatever you did was wrong. Since childhood was not a happy time, raising children can't help but bring back much of that unhappiness. It's not you, it's your memories, and the childhood you lived. You know the kind of parent you don't want to be, but you can't quite be the parent you want to be.

Relax. You can change all of that and redo your own childhood in the process. As you allow yourself to access those unhappy childhood memories, and consciously react differently to your child, you are undoing your childhood pain. What a wonderful opportunity to change your life now. You will no longer be enslaved by your past. You will be free, as a parent, to relate with compassion and understanding toward your family.

Now, how do I know that? I certainly don't know the intricacies of your childhood. But I do know that children blame themselves, not their parents, for what is wrong—because it's too frightening otherwise. If you were five years old, and you knew something was very wrong with your parents, would you be scared? What could you do? As a child, you needed to feel safe and protected. You knew that your life depended on your parents for very basic needs such as food, shelter, and clothing. If you thought your parents were unable to provide for you, it would have been too threatening. So you did as most of us do. You used your defense mechanisms to help you feel safe. You either denied that any problem existed, or you became responsible for the problem so that you could deal with it. You may have imagined a secret world where you felt safe and protected. You may have become a victim, and now you live with someone who is constantly blaming you. And, blaming yourself, you may be unable to move out of your circumstances. Or you may be an enabler who helps your spouse behave toward you and your children the way your parents behaved.

In any case, as a child, it was easier to blame yourself than your parents, because that belief allowed you to feel safe in your environment, even when it really wasn't so safe. With that memory lodged deeply in your mind, your child also can't do anything right. You may be overreacting to what he is doing today. It may be a case of mistaken identity. Your child may be receiving the unresolved anger or resentment that belongs to another time, place, and person.

Take the time to separate your child from this person by saying to yourself, "My child is not my…(name person). He is just a child, and didn't mean to do or say…" Repeat this phrase until it begins to appear automatically, in place of the other thought.

Now observe your child. Does she look different to you? Do you see what you couldn't have seen before? When you can do this, you will find the guidance here to be more helpful. After all, you will be reacting to your child, not to the person from your past or present who still upsets you. What a gift for both you and your child!

As Plato said, "An unexamined life is not worth living." By examining your life, and how you were raised, you have the opportunity to learn how to turn your negatives into positives, and your sabotages into successes. It will be your first step in *controlling your reactions*, and not having your reactions control you.

Learning to Control Your Reactions

Now that you realize that you may be reacting to your child the same way your parents reacted to you, there are six steps you can take to change this pattern. It takes work to become consciously aware of what is happening to you, and then, to change it. For example, when you decide to eat differently, or to exercise daily, it takes quite a commitment to put this into practice. But once you do, it feels so good. The right exercise and diet gives you a body you are proud to have. You must follow through on a task to get results. Make an impact on your life. Follow the six IMPACT steps to help you gain control of your reactions. Once you do, your life will be more fulfilling because you will react from knowledge and awareness, not from unconscious behavior.

● ● ●

IMPACT in Action

I—I

Acknowledge your feelings. When your child speaks or behaves toward you in a certain way, and you begin to feel angry, frustrated, anxious, or sad, acknowledge that your feelings are being violated. Say to yourself, "This feeling is not about my child. It is about me. This feeling is coming from how I felt as a child." Repeat this statement five times, or until you feel more relaxed.

M—My

Step out of your circumstances. Distance yourself for a moment either by mentally or physically leaving the situation. Ask yourself, "What am I feeling now—sad, scared, anxious, angry, frustrated? Where is this feeling coming from? What happened to me as a child when I was in this circumstance? How did my parents react or respond?"

Validate your feelings by saying, "I can see that little me is upset because..." Then empathize by saying, "I can imagine how awful this must have felt for little me when I was small, and alone." Next tell yourself, "I am here for you now. I will take care of you and be here for you."

P—Perception

Change it! Remember, if possible, the perception your parents had of you. Ask yourself, "What is my perception of my child right now? What statement am I making about my child? You're selfish. You're a spoiled brat. I never would have gotten away with that." Make a new positive statement about your child now.

A—Assumption

Ask yourself, "What assumption am I making about my child right now? Do I think she is selfish, spoiled, or bad?" Now, *change your assumption*. Tell yourself, "My child is not a brat. She is not spoiled. She is a good girl. Children have temper tantrums. I can help her instead of criticizing her as my parents criticized me."

Now, see your child for the innocent, loving being she is. She is only doing what a child in this situation has to do in order to get her needs met. Perhaps it is your attention she needs. Ask yourself why she is reacting this way, and if there is something that you can do for her.

Attitude

Ask yourself, "How are my emotions impacting my attitude? My child is not me. I am not my parents. My child has been raised in a different environment than I was raised in. My child will not need to turn out like ———. I am the parent, and I can react differently than my parents did. My child will grow up to be who he is."

C—Communication

How can you show your child a better way to handle this situation? First, you must be able to access your higher self and to see all of the goodness in your child. Ask yourself, "What is my child trying to tell me by reacting this way?" She may be helping you look at yourself as a child, but she is doing it differently than you did. What feelings are surfacing? You may feel angry, but it may be a better alternative than the one you chose as a child. Could you possibly envy her choice of behavior and secretly wish that you had the courage to express yourself the way she is?

T—Trust

Step into your child's world and imagine the feelings your child may be having at this moment. Then validate your child's feelings by saying, "I can see that you are upset because..." Then empathize by saying, "I can imagine that I would feel...too, if it were me. Would you tell me about it?"

• • •

After understanding both sides of the situation, the crisis will pass. As the parent, you will be in control and able to react in the way you wish, not in the way your parents reacted to you. A new acceptance will begin, and with it the seeds of communication— and a more satisfying relationship.

Chapter 3

Focus on What You Do Right

The Roles of Parents

Most of us believe our parents did a pretty good job of raising us and we're fine just the way we are. But if they had raised us in a really positive way, what more could we have been? I'm not telling you that you had bad parents. I am simply asking you to consider that there might have been a more positive way to help you reach your potential. What if your parents had continually focused on what you did right? Wouldn't that have helped you habitually do your best, instead of unconsciously sabotaging yourself in the many ways you do today? Wouldn't you have become a more confident person, one who is not afraid to make mistakes, but who looks forward to correcting errors and learning from them? Would you have to focus on being positive, or would that come naturally?

Your father's role in your life was equally as important as your mother's, and his presence or absence in your life contributed to your development. Fathers have a different kind of parenting to offer their children—a very logical way to view the world.

It has been said that mothers are there to nurture and protect their children, while fathers are there to reach into the mother's womb and bring their children out to meet the world. Each has a very different unconscious agenda as a parent.

These roles continue to change as parents learn how crucial it is to understand themselves, how the way they were parented affects their parenting ability, and how important is for them to nurture themselves so they can really be there for their children. Only then can they begin to truly understand their children and what problems they face daily.

Fathers are learning the value of letting their emotional, loving sides show, while mothers are still trying to be nurturing, protective, and loving. As fathers assume more of a role in parenting, more mothers than ever before are making their way in the business world. Both are learning the value of stepping outside of their roles to view what is happening.

I hope the stories in this book will be helpful to both mothers and fathers. I'm encouraged by the increasing role I see fathers play in parenting. This is a very difficult and challenging time to raise children. I hope this book will give you some needed insights and help along the way.

Knowing what to expect, and how to handle the unexpected makes all the difference. Principles, like our Bill of Rights, give us our freedom and standard of living. How we apply our principles in our daily lives separates one person from another. These standards set a structure for meeting the challenges we encounter daily. Once the basic foundation is set, our own creativity will surface to meet other difficulties as well.

Your Unconscious Agenda

In each of the twenty-six principles listed in the next section, look for your unconscious agenda. Become a detective and see your behavior as a clue to the way you were treated as a child. This book is meant to raise your awareness. It is not intended to make you feel guilty. It is meant to help you uncover your unconscious agenda—and then help you deal with it.

Be persistent. Instead of feeling guilty and blaming yourself for the way you interact with your child, use your feelings as a clue to discover what happened to you when you were the very same age. You are programmed like a computer. The way to pull up a specific file on the computer is to press the right keys. When a situation occurs in which you respond negatively, and without thinking, your unconscious agenda is surfacing. It was programmed a long time ago, and it is difficult to change. But you can do it. Be patient with yourself. You deserve to give yourself the best help you possibly can.

To change your program, you have to use your behavior as a clue. Ask yourself, "What did Mom or Dad do in that situation. How did they treat me when I didn't listen?" Talk about it. Chances are you are doing or saying exactly what was said or done to you. You will learn more about yourself than you could ever imagine. By becoming aware of why you act the way you do, your new responses will gradually become conscious. That is, you will be able to think first, and act second.

Each clue is a key to changing your present and becoming the parent you longed to have, and living in the family you dreamed about. Don't give up. Just follow the clues from your childhood. Abuse is cyclical. So is caring parenting.

Focus on What You Do Right

Now that you are aware, you can see that many things your child does access feelings from your childhood. You may be ready to look at three categories of principles that will help you and your children find a new beginning where you can focus on what you do right, not on what you do wrong. You may be ready to change your perception, and your assumptions, and truly step into your child's world. Your new ways of perceiving your child's behavior can help you begin to let go of past anger and resentment, and to react in the present.

Study these principles and abide by them. The twenty-six principles will help you:

1. Discover the rules for growing self-confidence.
2. Discover the unwritten laws that help you trust yourself and your children.
3. Develop discipline from the inside.

Mean what you say. Make your word your bond—and your life will be more enjoyable and present less conflict. Your children will do what you do, not what you tell them to do. Remember, they learn from your example. If you follow through on your actions, so will they. Enjoy the process—and watch yourself and your family grow.

Life isn't as easy as the ABCs, but mastering these twenty-six basic principles simplifies the task.

The Twenty-Six Principles

RULES FOR GROWING SELF-CONFIDENCE: PRINCIPLES I–IX

I. Gotcha!! Catch yourself and your kids doing things right—and give praise for it.
II. Mistakes are your teachers.
III. Praise yourself and your children for taking responsibility for mistakes.
IV. Accept and acknowledge yourself, so you can accept and acknowledge your children.
V. Respect your children and they will respect themselves.
VI. Perfection isn't the answer.
VII. Never do for your children what they can do for themselves.
VIII. Eliminate blame from your vocabulary.
IX. Say no to negativity.

LAWS THAT ENSURE TRUST BETWEEN YOU AND YOUR CHILD: PRINCIPLES X–XIX

Look for rules that either were or were not present in your family.

X. Say what you mean, and mean what you say.
XI. Follow through.
XII. The key to happiness is balance.
XIII. Talk about it because it won't go away.
XIV. Don't just "hear" what your children saying—"listen" to them.
XV. Talking about it is better than TV.
XVI. Never give up.
XVII. Go the extra mile.
XVIII. One thing at a time, and that done well.
XIX. Stories teach important lessons.

DISCIPLINE IS FROM THE INSIDE: PRINCIPLES XX–XXVI

Children do what you do, not what you tell them to do.

XX. Discuss, plan, and build in natural consequences before behavior breaks down.
XXI. A rule is a rule is a rule.
XXII. Don't just set boundaries—have agreed-on boundaries.
XXIII. Put your family agreements in writing.
XXIV. Be willing to give up something to accomplish the larger goal.
XXV. Negotiate.
XXVI. Let your children win the battles, you win the war.

Why You React the Way You Do

As part of each principle, there will be questions that you might want to answer. These questions are there to jog your memory. When you find yourself overreacting or responding to your child in a way that you are not proud of (that is, blaming or shaming your child), accept and acknowledge that it wasn't your intention to behave that way. If you could have, you would have responded differently. Your response was probably an unconscious reaction to what your child did.

For most of us, our children bring up feelings that we don't recognize until it is too late. Most likely, it was a case of mistaken identity. Your child's behavior brought back a remembered feeling from your childhood. When this happens, and you do not have time to go through the steps outlined previously to gain control of your reactions, simply take five deep breaths, holding each breath in your stomach to the count of five. Then relax again by breathing out, counting backward from five. This should bring you into a state of deep relaxation.

Now allow yourself to go back to the age that your child is now. Let yourself feel what it was like being a child of that age living in your parents' home. Was it relaxed, happy, anxious, or tense? How did your caretakers react to you when you did what your child is doing now? Compare what happened to you with the situation you just overreacted to. Did you react to your child the way your parent reacted to you, or did you react in a totally opposite way? As you revisit your earlier childhood, memories will begin to reappear and the answers will come.

Each principle and story will remind you of feelings from your past. Allow them to reappear for you. As you recall what happened as a child, your parenting will improve. Each memory will be an opportunity for you to revisit what it was like to be a child, and will help you perceive what your young child may be feeling today.

As these feelings surface, you will become freer and more aware. You are beginning to travel the road to emotional awareness. Your memories will help you understand why you are reacting the way you do. Knowledge is powerful. With it, you can begin to change. Without it, nothing changes.

A Word of Caution: Please read only one principle a week—just one. This practice will help you digest it, practice it, and begin to make it part of your life. Of course, it's easier said than done. Take your time. It will be worthwhile. As you become more interested in specific details of the childhood stages in which you were wounded, you may want to read *Giving the Love That Heals*, by Harville Hendrix, Ph.D.

Part One

~

Rules for Growing Self-Confidence

~

Principles I–IX

~ Chapter 4 ~

Principle I.

Gotcha! Catch Yourself and Your Kids Doing Things Right— and Give Praise for It

Do you remember either of your parents, or caretakers, focusing on what you did right? Did they stop you during an argument with your brother and say, "I like the way you spoke to Johnny. It helped him understand why you were so angry." Or did they say, "Now Johnny is younger than you, and he doesn't understand. You have to give in because you're the older brother. Don't be selfish. Let him have his way." Would you have remembered the scolding, or the compliment? Which statement would have helped you feel confident and in control of the situation?

Focus on What You and Your Children Do Right

Because you were used to being criticized as a child, you may have incorporated self-criticism into your personality. For example, "I should have stood up for myself. Why did I keep my mouth shut, and let my boss berate me like that?" Or perhaps you were blamed for whatever went wrong in your house. Does your spouse often say, "You blame me for everything. It is always my fault." Because of what happened in your childhood home, you probably either criticized yourself, or blamed others, and now you may be in a pattern of behavior that is difficult to change. But it isn't too late, as long as you want to change. The secret is to focus on what you do right. It won't take you long to "get it." Develop the habit of noticing the little things you do right, and praise yourself for them. It will help you see the good in yourself, and also the good in others. Self-praise can give you the confidence to improve and overcome your bad habits.

When you spilled milk, did your mom yell, "You bad boy. You should be ashamed of yourself." Did you clean it up or run away? Did your mother become angrier? How did you feel about yourself?

The other day one of my son's thirty-year-old friends spilled beer while I was serving food. Instead of apologizing or helping me clean up, he walked away as quickly as he could. It may have been that I knocked the glass over, but he was so frightened by the situation, I never found out. What do you think happened to him when he was little?

What if when you spilled milk at the dinner table, your mom hadn't yelled? Let's say, instead she took a deep breath, and said to herself, "Inner calm, inner calm. It's only milk. The world didn't end." And then she said to you, "You were in such a hurry to finish your meal, you accidentally knocked the milk over. I know you'll clean it up right away, and I'll help if you need it. And by the way, I like the way you are starting to eat slowly. I'm proud of you." How proud would you have felt? Would you have cleaned up? Would you have taken your time at the next meal?

What if you decide to treat your children the way you would have liked your parents to treat you? Will that help you become aware of the way you treat yourself? Will it make it easier for you to forgive yourself the next time you make a "stupid" mistake? When positive thinking becomes natural, you'll feel more relaxed and learn how to take your time. You won't resent helping your child clean up because you'll feel proud of how you helped her.

Your children will remember your confidence in them, and their self-confidence will soar.

By the way, I didn't say it would be easy. It's much easier to react as our parents did. As an adult, when I thought about my parents, I remembered all of the good things they did. But when I reacted to my children by hurrying, yelling, or not listening, I knew my parents must have been that way toward me. Change is difficult. It was for me, but it was equally rewarding.

The Consequences of Focusing on Mistakes

Let's look at what happened to you when your parents only focused on what you did wrong: Whenever you did something your mother didn't like, did she say, "Wait until your father comes home!" Were you so scared of what he would do that you spent the entire day in your room worrying about it? When Dad came home, lots of times he didn't do anything. But the damage was done; your fear of him and your worry about what he would do stayed with you, even when you were much older.

You probably were most afraid of your father's judging you: What if he thought you were bad? Would he still love you? You were too scared of him to think about it, or risk talking about it. So you began to think it was better not to tell him anything. As you grew older, did not telling Dad change into lying? Lying was easier than facing your mother's threats or your father's anger. You got to do what you wanted to do, as long as no one found out. The trouble was that you probably spent so much time worrying about what others thought, you never really got to know what you thought. It was too risky. What if others didn't approve? Now, do you spend the majority of your time pleasing others, so you'll be sure they love you?

The consequences can be severe; you never learn to stand up for your own beliefs. Judgment prevents you from learning to enjoy your life. If you spend your life just pleasing others, it isn't much fun.

The power of positive parenting can move mountains. Teach your children by example. While they are young, and as they continue to grow, help them see that they have the power to reach their finest potential.

Look to the child within you, and focus on what you do right, while you are learning to respond in the same way toward your children.

Joan, a successful businesswoman, said, "As a child, I was more concerned about learning how to do what I could do, rather than what I did wrong, or lying about what I did. When I said, 'I can't do it,' Mom showed me how I could. I became more and more confident as I mastered each new task. I remember when I learned to say, "I can, I can, I can. I did it." It was just like that story she read to me, *The Little Engine That Could*. I suggest that you read it to your children, over and over. It can become part of who they are. When they can't do something, encourage them to try again. Help them to help themselves.

Let Your Children See You Struggle

Allow your children the privilege of seeing you struggle with a project, and your willingness to try again until you succeed. Compliment yourself for it. Focus on what your children do right, and point it out to them. "I like the way you handled your friend. I wish I had been able to do that." Or, "You thought you couldn't write that paper and it turned out to be your best one yet." Stick to the truth. Kids have a way of knowing when we make up behaviors or feelings. When we do that they trust us less.

Your positive comments will go a long way. They are food for your child's soul. Watch how your children emulate you. My children would ask me to do something I really thought couldn't be done, and then insist that I could do it. Because of what I had said to them, I felt obligated to try again, especially when they said, "You can do it, Mom, you can do it." Even when I failed, they kept encouraging me. And to my surprise, I succeeded. Watch what you say to your children—your words might come back to you!

*People are always blaming circumstances for what
they are. I do not believe in circumstances.
The people who get on in this world are the people
who get up and look for the circumstances they
want, and if they cannot find them, make them.*

GEORGE BERNARD SHAW
IRISH PLAYWRIGHT (1856–1950)

IMPACT Story: Patrick

At age five, Patrick did what he wanted to do when he wanted to
do it, and only listened when it suited him. He established a reputation in school as a child who did not listen. Even when he wanted
to do what he was told to do, he was perceived negatively by his
teachers. Patrick was locked in a vicious cycle, and didn't have any
idea of how to break it. Without major changes, he was on a path
of self-destruction. His parents were frightened for the future.

Mary, Patrick's mother, wanted to understand him and to
help him react differently to his world. She worried that he would
turn out like his uncle who blamed everyone but himself for his
problems and was constantly in trouble.

John, Patrick's father, was totally frustrated with the situation. He wanted to be a good father, but he lost patience when Pat
taunted and teased at the dinner table instead of behaving appropriately. When John slapped Patrick, Mary became very angry.
She did not agree with John's tactics. He said, "I'm forty-two
years old, he's five. I have to go to his level?"

John was doing what his father had done to him. When Mary
pointed that out, he said, "I don't want my son to remember me
as I remember my father. But I just don't know how to get
through to him." John didn't like the way he was handling Patrick,
but he knew no other way. Mary and John agreed they needed to
find a better solution for this very difficult and painful situation.
Sending Pat to his room, or giving him a time-out, just didn't
work. When Pat returned to the table, his behavior was worse
than before. When sent to his room, he played with all of his

favorite toys and had a wonderful time. The next day, he would replay the same scene at dinner.

John tried to talk to Patrick calmly, "Patrick, don't annoy everyone during dinner." Patrick only laughed and began making faces. John quickly reacted by saying, "Don't you mock me." And so the power struggle began. John's repertoire of behavior was used up. He knew one way to react—his father's way. But with one exception—John spoke nicely to Patrick before he got angry. Since John's dad was always angry, John thought he was way ahead of the game. He only smacked Patrick as a last resort.

When Patrick went to school the day after the incident, he was constantly in trouble. His teacher asked him why he was so angry. Patrick said, "Wouldn't you be angry if your parents always yelled at each other?" Patrick was a smart boy. He might have been misbehaving at the dinner table as a way of diverting attention away from his parents' anger at each other. He just didn't have the right words to express his feelings, so he spoke with his actions. And it worked.

Mary hated the anger in the house. She remembered it all too clearly from her own childhood, but she didn't know how to stop it. As she saw the cycle repeating itself in her new family, she had reason to worry. Fortunately both Mary and John were willing to learn a better way to communicate and relate to each other. So instead of going out to dinner every week, John and Mary invested that time and money in their family—through counseling. Both parents committed to following through. "Our children deserve that much from us," John said. They wanted to get rid of the anger in their home, and were able to acknowledge that it was what they had each lived with as children. They knew it wouldn't be easy to change the patterns they were repeating from their childhood, but they weren't ready to divorce either. Life was so frustrating that it just wasn't fun anymore. But they loved their children too much *not* to try.

As they expressed their feelings in counseling, Mary and John began to see that Patrick's anger was a reflection of their own anger. Mary commented, "Patrick treats his sister the way you treat him. The other day he said, 'Eat your cereal or I'll get in there, and I'll give you what you need—a good whack.' Do you want him to act like that to his sister?" It wasn't long before they realized that if they got rid of their anger, Patrick would calm down. They began to track their own discord, and Patrick's behavior. To their surprise, their fights and Pat's misbehavior at school coincided. When both parents had a good day or weekend at home, Patrick's behavior improved at school. It was a good sign, but John and Mary knew they had a lot of work ahead of them. The most valuable advice the counselor gave them was to never give up, and to follow through. They were aware that their patterns, caused by a lifetime of unhappiness, couldn't be changed in a few weeks or months.

John decided to meet Patrick at his level instead of trying to control him by being angry and hostile, just as his own father had been. That meant being firm with Patrick and setting consequences for behavior in advance. When Patrick didn't respond to John, he took both of Patrick's hands, held them firmly in his, looked Patrick right in the eye, and said, "Patrick, you can sit calmly at the dinner table with us. If you feel we are angry, then just tell us. We will listen. You do your part, and we will do ours. You are a good boy, and you *can listen*." John was surprised when Patrick responded positively. And when Patrick behaved, John told him how proud he was. "I like the way you are behaving tonight. I am enjoying having my dinner with you." John wasn't the only one who was surprised. What about Patrick?

John began to tell Patrick what he did right, and made a point of catching him at it. Then he rewarded Patrick's behavior with a compliment, and sometimes with an extra bedtime story, or a game of catch after dinner. John said, "It works. It really does! Patrick listens to me when I compliment him. And I have been catching him doing so many things right, that when he makes a mistake, he expresses his view, I express mine, and we seem to meet each other halfway. That's more than I ever expected. It really is working."

• • •

IMPACT in Action

I—I
"I did what I was told to do or I got it. I felt lucky when I did not get hit."

M—My
"My feelings weren't considered. They didn't count."

P—Perception
"Patrick is a brat. He never listens and he does just what he wants to do. I never could have gotten away with that."

A—Assumption
"He is just trying to control me."

Attitude
"What am I doing that's impacting Patrick's behavior? He is a good boy, and he's very smart. I am going to focus on his good qualities, and not see him as bad, the way my parents saw me.

"I know Patrick doesn't like it when my wife and I fight. It upsets him. He really is as sensitive as I was as a child. I used to hate it when Dad yelled. I thought it was my fault when Mom yelled back. Patrick may be misbehaving just to prevent us from fighting. And it's working. Now that we realize how much it bothers him, we are not arguing as much. Patrick's not bad. He's just reacting to what he's feeling, the only way he can do it as a child."

C—Communication
"I'll have a talk with Patrick. I'll tell him I understand that he might be upset because Mom and I are fighting so much. I remember what it was like for me. Maybe we can agree that he can tell Mom or me whenever he is upset rather than acting out. I'll tell him that we are also trying to communicate better, and that we need him to express his feelings, rather than act out."

T—Trust
"I'll set up a reward system to help Patrick express his feelings instead of acting out. Patrick will enjoy being praised for good behavior. I'll trust Patrick to find a reward we both agree on, and in the process we will both learn how to express our feelings."

~ **Chapter 5** ~

Principle II.
Mistakes Are Your Teachers

It can become fun to correct mistakes when you do not get anxious about them; that is, when you take "perfect" out of your vocabulary and replace it with "challenge."

Discovering how you grow from your mistakes can become a friendly contest in your home. Don't make a big thing out of a little mistake; instead, look for what can be learned from it. After a while everyone will joke about it—watch and see how it helps. Encourage an atmosphere of lightness and levity. Growth comes from learning what you can do, not what you can't do; and from finding out how to change what you do so you won't make the same mistake again.

When you feel confident about making and correcting mistakes, you won't be afraid to tackle more difficult tasks. Do you remember the first time you fell off your bicycle? Did you feel like giving up? Did you feel bad about making that mistake? Didn't you try again? And how did you feel when you discovered how not to fall, and when you had the confidence to know it's okay to fall?

How would you guide your child? When she doesn't feel ashamed of falling off her bike, won't she be less anxious to ask you to show her how to find the balance she's looking for?

When you believe mistakes are your teachers because you learn from them, you will relax. This belief will give you the independence to experiment, and try new things. Experiment and try it in just one area of your life. When you can adopt this attitude, your children will absorb it, and the positive challenges it presents as well.

Learning from Your Mistakes: Sue's Story

Let's look at what happened to Sue when she made a mistake. When Sue accidentally knocked over a vase of flowers, she was so scared that she'd be punished that she tried to cover it up. Of course, her mother discovered what had happened and sent Sue to her room, even more angry at her daughter because she'd tried to hide the broken vase.

What if Sue's mother had given her a sponge instead, and said, "I'll help you clean this up. Next time you're racing around the house, you'll think about being more careful. That way, when you make a mistake and correct it, I'll feel proud of you instead of becoming angry." Would that have helped Sue feel better and gain control over what she did? We develop self-esteem by turning our small failures into successes.

Learning Patience: Barry's Story

We also need to help ourselves and our children develop patience. We can get what we want, but not always when we want it. Do you remember wanting a new toy, or ice cream now? Do you remember how difficult it was to wait? When you learned to wait, you learned patience as well. So what if you or your children make a mistake by doing things at the wrong time. That's how you learn. It might have saved you from making a bigger mistake later on.

Let's see what happened to Barry when he wanted his father to help him *now* with his model car. His father didn't yell or just say no. The key was, his father knew that he must talk about the consequences before they happen so that Barry would have the experience of understanding why this was not a good time to begin a project. Although his father wanted to work with him on the engine, it was too close to dinner to get started.

> **Dad:** *I'd really like to help you with this engine, Barry, but it's only thirty minutes until dinner, and I don't think we'll have time. Let's wait until Saturday.*
>
> **Barry:** *I want to do it now. I can't wait until Saturday.*
>
> **Dad:** *That does seem like a long time, and I know it is not easy to wait. I used to hate that too. But what if you start the engine, and can't finish it?*
>
> **Barry:** *I'll finish without you.*
>
> **Dad:** *It looks too difficult to do alone.*
>
> **Barry:** *I can do it. Don't worry! I'm going to do it now, anyway.*
>
> **Dad:** *Okay, it's your choice. But will you come to dinner when Mom calls?*
>
> **Barry:** *Sure.*
>
> **Dad:** *What if you're not finished, or you do need my help?*
>
> **Barry:** *Then I'll do it after dinner.*
>
> **Dad:** *That's great, but I'm wondering how you'll do your homework also?*
>
> **Barry:** *I will, you'll see.*
>
> **Dad:** *Okay, but if your homework isn't done, and you're not in bed on time, we'll have to put off our bike ride tomorrow. Is that okay with you?*
>
> **Barry:** *No, I don't want to put it off.*
>
> **Dad:** *Everything has its consequence—no homework, no biking. You decide. But don't complain afterward. Okay?*

Barry: nods.
Dad: If the choice you make doesn't turn out the way you wanted, you'll learn from it. Then you can start fresh tomorrow. Okay?
Barry: Sure, Dad, I get it.

Barry pays the penalty, not his father. How else will he learn? How did you learn? The promised consequences should occur regardless of protests. Barry knows his father will follow through. His father is aware Barry realizes it, so there is little likelihood of Barry throwing a temper tantrum or his father indulging in "I told you so." Everything has been explained up-front—that makes the difference. Which approach did your parents take?

Where there is great doubt, there will be great awakening; small doubt, small awakening; no doubt, no awakening.

ZEN SAYING

Chapter 6

Principle III.

Praise Yourself and Your Children for Taking Responsibility for Mistakes

When you praise yourself and your children for admitting mistakes, you are teaching both of you not to lie, and how to be responsible. Most children lie because they get into trouble when they tell the truth. Do you remember your first lie? What made you do it?

Praise Your Children for Admitting Their Mistakes

Suppose your child came in from the backyard covered with dirt? Would you yell, or would you ask what happened? Suppose your three-year-old was proud of the hole he had dug right where you had planted the daffodils? What would you do then? What you do sets a precedent for how he'll respond next time he does something wrong. If he gets into trouble telling the truth, he'll remember it, and the next time he'll lie. What happened to you?

What if you asked him why he dug that hole and he said, "I saw you digging in the garden last week, and I wanted to do it too." That makes logical sense for a three-year-old. Then your best response would be, "When I dug a hole in the garden, I planted daffodils. But when you dug a hole, you didn't plant seeds, and if we dig holes everywhere, we'll have a messy looking backyard. If you want to help, I'll let you dig holes and plant seeds in them when we are both in the garden together, so I can show you where to make the holes. If you don't want to plant seeds, you can dig holes in your sandbox, or at the beach when I take you."

At this point it is best to praise your child for telling the truth. He knew by the look on your face that he had done something wrong. You can say, "I'm proud of you for telling the truth. I won't punish you for digging holes because I know you did what you thought was a good thing. Next time, would you ask first, so I can tell you if it is okay? That way I won't get angry, and you won't get into trouble. It will be a good way to learn. Won't it?"

Of course you wouldn't give all this information at once to your three-year old, but you might to a six-year-old.

Can you see how he is learning to be responsible, honest, and truthful? What if you had yelled and punished him? What would he discover then? Wouldn't you be setting up a power struggle?

Praising your children for admitting their mistakes gives them tools that develop self-confidence. If you were praised instead of scolded when you did something wrong, would you be more confident and more able to be responsible for your actions today? What if you felt proud when you corrected your mistakes instead of ashamed of making them? We all make mistakes, don't we?

Accept Responsibility for Your Mistakes

Another way to demonstrate this principle is to accept and admit your own errors to your children. What better way could they learn to take responsibility, and trust you?

Sometimes your children are upset by a mistake you made, but they can't always express it in words. Tina wouldn't go to bed, and no matter what her mother did, she kept screaming. She was driving her father crazy, but he knew she was crying for a reason. He chose to try to understand rather than reprimand her. When he asked, Tina told him, "I don't want to go to sleep. When I wake up you'll be gone like you were when you left me in the car today." Her father was surprised. He hadn't realized how much fear this incident caused. "I made a mistake. I will never leave you in the car alone again. I was gone for a minute and I didn't think you would wake up. But you're right. It was not a safe thing for me to do. I'm sorry you were scared that I left you, and I promise I won't do that again. Will you forgive me?" Tina said okay and went straight to sleep. Children can be very forgiving.

When her father took responsibility for his mistake, Tina relaxed and began to trust him again. He also showed her what she could do when she made a mistake. Her lesson was, "Even fathers make mistakes. I know he loves me now, and I forgive him." When Tina makes a mistake, will she be able to admit it and also forgive herself? Tina had the courage to tell her father the real truth because she had experienced his honesty before. Your example will help your children not to fear mistakes and to take responsibility for them, just as they see you do. Would you appreciate being responded to in that way? Learning can be effortless when the fear of doing things wrong is gone, and making them right is fun.

Vow to see the best in yourself and your children; both of you will rise to your expectations. The victory will be yours.

Show your children you believe in them and they will believe in themselves. So Tom spilled on the new rug. So what? Tell him you know he'll do a good job cleaning it up, and watch him do it. If he needs help, then help him—as long as you don't do it for him. When your children mess up, tell them, "I know you can fix this problem." Count on it. Offer help, and watch them rise to the occasion. Tell yourself the same things.

Be there for your children when they're young, and help them accomplish their goals. Don't wait until they are teenagers. By then, their feelings about whether or not they can do it are already formed. They're confident if you've been proud of them when they achieved small goals along the way. When your children are teenagers, they will be on their own. Will they have to do what other kids do such as too much drinking or drugs? What have they done all of their lives? Who made their decisions when they were younger? The more experience they have, the more confident they become, and the better able they are to choose wisely. The more you are behind them, the more able they are to be there for themselves.

Your children will need to earn money, and learn the value of waiting and saving for things. When your children know you are on their side helping them earn what they want, they'll develop the ability to wait for things, and the confidence to know they'll achieve their goals.

The Chinese say a trip of a thousand miles begins with the *first step*. And the first step is the first step. When your child is three years old, it means helping him clean up a mess, or her choose between a peanut butter-and-jelly, or tuna sandwich. At four, it's about which toys to share, and why he has to share. At five, it's which child should she invite over for play. If your child wants to build the tallest sandcastle possible, help him; just don't do it for him. He'll be able to build the next sandcastle by himself with the confidence you gave him. The choices get more complicated, but the ability to make them improves with experience. Don't say, "I told you so!" Tell yourself and your children, "It's okay to make mistakes. You learn from them." Help both of you not to give up, and to learn from your mistakes. Achieving goals and learning from your mistakes can become a natural part of your life, and will help you to choose more wisely as time goes by.

> *Begin difficult things while they are easy,*
> *do great things when they are small.*
> *The difficult things of the world must once have*
> *been easy;*
> *the great things must once have been small...*
> *A thousand mile journey begins with one step.*
>
> LAO-TSE
> CHINESE PHILOSOPHER, 6TH CENTURY B.C.

Teach Your Children to Be Responsible for Their Mistakes

When our children make mistakes, we do not own their mistakes. They are their mistakes, not ours. It is important that we separate ownership from responsibility. Our children are responsible for their own behavior. As parents we are responsible for teaching and guiding them to understand and acknowledge their behavior and to see consequences for what they do. The best we can do is to allow our children their mistakes, and to guide them so they can profit from what they have learned.

The Importance of Common Sense

Common sense is when you know what, when, and how to do what you are doing. Knowing what, when, and how comes from having the experience of doing. If we do not guide our children to learn from their mistakes, and we punish and shame them instead, what are we accomplishing? How will they know what is right and wrong, and what to do and what not to do?

We need to give our children lots of experience when they are little and are receptive to our guidance and love, to help them develop common sense and intuition as they grow older. We have a very limited time in which to teach and guide them. When they become teenagers, they "have" to do it for themselves.

Doesn't the generation gap begin when our children will not listen to us anymore? As teenagers, they insist on doing it "their way." Therefore parental influence diminishes measurably. Also, as they spend time away from us, they need to make good choices.

We still have authority, and we can choose to use it either by guiding them or by controlling them. "It's my life, not yours" is a familiar phrase. What did you do when you were a teenager? The more control your parents used over you, the more you rebelled. The more experience you had in making decisions, the more you were able to make decisions that put you in a positive direction.

Was it easy or hard for you? Did you follow your friends and do what they did in order to belong? Were you tired of all the rules and of your parents telling you what to do? Or did you do what you thought was right, and walk away from situations that put you in jeopardy? Even when those decisions were difficult for you, how did you know when to follow your friends and when not to? You may have been one of the lucky ones who had lots of experience making mistakes, and had parents who were readily available to exchange ideas with you. If so, by this age, you may have developed common sense.

IMPACT Story: Bob

When Bob was growing up, Sarah, his mother, wouldn't allow him to do anything on his own. She controlled him because of her own childhood fears. Sarah worried that Bob would turn out like her sister who was always in trouble.

In order to fight his mother's control, and armed with little experience of making decisions on his own, Bob walked into his teenage years rebelliously, and into one bad situation after another. For the first time, Sarah could no longer control his every move.

When he found himself with friends who were experimenting with drugs, Bob hadn't developed enough common sense to walk away, or enough inner security to say no. It looked like fun, so he went for it. For the first time in his life, he was in control. Alone in the world and unprepared to make intelligent and mature decisions, Bob was destined to fail. He didn't understand that his behavior would entail consequences. He had little understanding of cause and effect.

As he grew older, Bob graduated from doing drugs to selling them, to stealing radios, electronic equipment, and to vandalism, like smashing windows on Halloween. And usually Bob was caught. His answer was always the same, "I didn't do it. My friends ran away. I was here when the cops came." The track Bob was on led to anger at society, incarceration, and fear of what would happen next.

Bob was really a good boy until the rules at home became harder and harder to follow. Understandably, he needed to find an outlet from the oppression. What if he had had a patient mother who had guided him through his mistakes, without using punitive control? Suppose Bob had learned to feel proud of correcting his errors? Would he have chosen a different road as a teenager? Would he have developed enough common sense, then and now, to discern right from wrong? And how about understanding consequences? What's your opinion?

● ● ●

IMPACT in Action

Let's look at the impact of control on Bob's emotional life.

I—I
"I have to live my own life." No one could change Bob's feeling that he had to do what he wanted to do, not what his mother wanted him to do.

M—My
"My feelings count." Bob kept saying over and over, "It's my life, not yours, Mom." But it didn't feel that way to Bob.

P—Perception
Bob perceived his life as if he lived in a prison. He thought that he was always in a no-win situation. If he didn't listen to his mother, she would be angry and ground him. He couldn't wait until he could get away from her control and be free at last. That's all he could think of. He said, "I'm going to do what I want to do now, not what my mom wants me to do. It's my life, not hers."

A—Assumption
Bob *assumed* that he knew what to do, and how to do it. He didn't realize that he had little experience in making his own decisions.

When his friends smashed windows on Halloween, Bob couldn't think of what to do. Part of him knew that he shouldn't run away. Another part knew that it was wrong to smash windows.

After Bob worked to pay for the windows and his court costs, his mother became even stricter than before. He now had to account for almost every minute of his time. Bob now assumed that there was no way to find his much desired freedom, but he couldn't give up. He was just like a plant that cannot stop reaching toward the sun, even if it gets twisted in the process.

Attitude

Now, Bob's *attitude* was that he had no freedom, and life wasn't fair. Instead of learning from his mistakes, his anger caused him to rebel even more. Getting into trouble, but doing it "his way" became a way of life.

C—Communication

Bob knew he had to change the way he was living his life. But he didn't know how. He didn't have any experience in doing it his way. By this time his mother realized that Bob wasn't going to listen to her. Feeling hopeless, she threw him out of the house.

At sixteen, with no experience in making and correcting his own mistakes, Bob was living on his own. Somehow his mother thought he would learn the hard way. And Bob did learn. He learned to lie, sell drugs, and manipulate everyone he met in order to find a place to live and some warm shelter. When he was tired, and defeated, he went home more ashamed than ever and pleading for his mother's forgiveness. He decided that he would obey the rules this time, and did for a while until she became overbearing again, and the cycle began anew.

T—Trust

What if Sarah had trusted Bob to make his own mistakes when he was little, to learn from them? And in the process, what if she had given him some control over his life? Wouldn't it have been easier if he had freedom to choose his own friends, and to make a mess in the house? Wouldn't cleaning up after himself have been a logical conse-quence, rather than being sent to his room and being told he couldn't play with his friend anymore? All the control issues Bob faced as a child gave him little experience, and little knowledge of how to act in the world as an adult.

• • •

IMPACT in Action

Let's look at Bob's mother, Sarah, and the feelings she grew up incorporating into her life.

I—I
"I'm not important. I have to do what I'm told or I'll get beaten."

M—My
"My feelings don't count. Other people count more."

P—Perception
Sarah was reliving the nightmare of her childhood through her son. She couldn't separate her son's childhood from her own. Sarah perceived her son as her sister.

Sarah's perception of the world was that children do what they're told; if they don't listen, they're severely punished. As a child, Sarah's job included cleaning the house, and caring for her younger sister. When her sister was "bad," and didn't listen, Sarah was punished, not her sister. Sarah's perception was that the world wasn't fair, and she communicated that to her son.

A—Assumption.
Although Sarah loved her son, she also *assumed* that he would turn out like her sister, or like the men she knew. Sarah's method for preventing her worst fear was to rule her son with an iron fist and watch his every move. Sarah's mother had left parenting up to Sarah who was only a child herself. Sarah wanted to make certain she didn't fail with her son as she felt she had failed with her sister.

Attitude
Sarah *hated* her younger sister because of the trouble she always managed to get her into. She hated her father who left her mother with four children to raise, and no money; and she hated her grandfather, the abusive alcoholic who lived with them. Sarah grew up hating men, and being frightened by them. She reacted to her son with anger and fear because of her childhood attitudes.

C—Communication

When Sarah communicated with her son, there was anger in her voice. Her fear was so overwhelming she felt that she had to always control him, even when he was very little, so that he wouldn't turn out like her sister.

Bob might have been a submissive child who listened to exactly what his mother said. But, by nature, Bob was rebellious. The way his mother treated him just didn't feel right, and, contrary to her beliefs, brought even more rebellion.

T—Trust

By not trusting herself, or her son, Sarah inadvertently caused her worst fears to come true. She kept thinking that Bob's life was her life, not an uncommon perception. Separating their lives was extremely difficult at times. But Bob didn't grow up in the same environment Sarah had. Sarah had not recognized that important distinction.

When Sarah was little, she was expected to parent her sister. As a child she couldn't fulfill that role. How many kids could? Nonetheless, Sarah felt that she had failed her sister. As an adult, Sarah's failure was in not being able to separate her son's life from herself. The saddest part is that Sarah hadn't been able to learn from her mother's mistakes because it was too overwhelming for a child to be in the position of a parent. Cruel and unfair, the cycle repeated itself, causing another round of suffering.

● ● ●

Don't you think Sarah's attitude had a profound impact on her son? Sarah wasn't aware that she abused her son emotionally by being too smothering, and then abandoning him to the streets when he didn't conform. She might say it was genetics. What do you think? Although Bob was rebellious, good parenting skills might have given his natural tendencies a positive direction. He might have had the potential to be a leader. Do you think the environment played a large role in Bob's life, or was it strictly genetics?

Chapter 7

Principle IV.

Accept and Acknowledge Yourself, So You Can Accept and Acknowledge Your Children

Your greatest challenge will be to discover how you can become accepting of yourself. When you embrace your strengths and weaknesses, you will recognize that you have them for a reason— to help you grow. They are opportunities and challenges to becoming the best you can be.

It is difficult to accept yourself for who you are especially when almost everyone you have encountered has pointed out your mistakes. The ones who encouraged and influenced you are your most trusted guides on your journey. It will take great strength, courage, and perseverance. Only when you can accept yourself, by understanding your mistakes and how to learn and grow from them, will you be able to do the same for your children. The gift of self-knowledge can be the greatest gift of all. For example, if you are a writer, and your child is an athlete, acknowledge and praise that ability in your child. If you are a carpenter, and your child wants to be an artist, accept and praise that ambition. Only then will your child feel truly loved and accepted.

Many parents might refuse to allow their children to pursue their interests. Now, what does that accomplish? Their children might do what they say, and hate them for it. After all, the parents made the choice, not them. How did you feel when your parents acted that way toward you? Do you still remember it?

Learn to Accept Yourself

Let's see how Bonnie treated herself. Even though she was late for an appointment, because it had taken longer to remove the ice from her car than she'd anticipated, Bonnie decided to take her time, relax, and enjoy the drive. When she reached into her pocket, the car keys weren't there. Trying not to panic, she checked her other pocket, and then her briefcase. She checked three times. The keys definitely weren't there. Then the old childhood feelings returned. As she rushed back to the house looking for her keys, she thought, "What's the matter with me? I can't believe I lost my keys. I'm never gonna make it. I'm so stupid. I always mess up."

When Bonnie was little, it is likely that when she made a mistake, one of her parents called her "stupid." If Bonnie is still talking that way to herself, can you imagine what she will say to her children if they lose their keys? When she is upset, she immediately begins criticizing herself. Why wouldn't she be the same way with her children?

Bonnie's husband had also had a bad day and was pretty grouchy at dinner. When Bonnie asked what was bothering him, his first response was to snap at her. Then he said to himself, "It's not my fault or Bonnie's that I am upset. So I had a bad day. Doesn't everyone at one time or another? I have to give myself a break." He turned to his wife, and said, "I had a really awful day, and need time to relax. I'm sorry for snapping. I'd like to calm down now. Maybe we can talk about it later, after I've given myself some space." Do you think it is likely that his parents explained their feelings to him when he was little? How do you think he will respond when his children are out-of-sorts and grouchy? Will he be able to help them understand their day or will he snap at them?

When you're able to understand why you were nasty at dinner, and accept that something is bothering you, it'll be equally as easy to wonder why your children are irritable, and ask them about their day.

Your children mirror your behavior. If you criticize yourself, your children will learn to criticize themselves as well. Even if you think your self-criticism is hidden, your children sense it and react to it on a nonverbal level. They pick up your energy, whether it is positive or negative. When you can acknowledge and accept that you have faults, your children will learn how to accept their faults as well. Accepting your faults, rather than denying them, will help you and your children be more relaxed about who you are. Therefore acceptance and acknowledgment of yourself is crucial to how you treat your children and how they learn to treat themselves. A good way to begin this process is to ask questions first. It will help you not to take your child's anger personally. After all, what happened is really not about you; most likely, it is about your child.

It takes lots of time and patience to become accepting of yourself, and to become aware of how your parents reacted to you, and why you are reacting to your child negatively. When you think about it, you may either be behaving in the same way as your parents, or in a totally opposite way. You will not be free to be you until you accept that who you are is really okay. Then you can acknowledge what you are doing that isn't working, and what you must do to change it. It's quite a task, and not one accomplished in a short time.

Ask Questions First: Portia's Story

Portia, a teacher, tried to be perfect, so much so that when anything went wrong, she blamed herself. Portia was in the habit of blaming herself because when she was little everyone kept telling her what she did wrong, and she took it seriously. Now if one of her children was sad, angry, or fresh, she would wonder what she had done wrong. When her son, Barry, was five, and at a challenging stage, she would say to herself, "Why is he such a brat?

Why is he trying to hurt me?" One weekend her husband watched the children while she worked. She missed her family a lot, and on her way home, she pictured herself giving each one a big hug. But as soon as she opened the door, Barry was nasty to her. She felt so angry that she walked out of the room again to give herself time alone, just to think about what had happened. After taking several deep breaths, she asked herself, "What did I do this time?" When she realized she couldn't have done anything wrong because she simply hadn't been around, she was able to separate her behavior from her son's.

She walked straight to Barry's room, and asked him what was wrong. Tears welled up in his eyes, his lips began to quiver, and he burst out crying, "Peter (his brother) wouldn't share his spaghetti with me. He ate it all. When I asked Dad if I could cook more, he yelled at me. Peter said he didn't do it, and Dad believed him."

To Portia's surprise, Barry's anger wasn't about her. And at that moment she learned an important truth, "I would have blamed myself for Barry's anger. But when I gave myself time to walk away, breathe deeply, and ask the right questions, I learned that it wasn't about me, it was about him. Barry was angry and hurt. I would never have learned about it if I hadn't asked. Why do I always blame myself first, and take things personally rather than ask questions?"

If Portia had been able to acknowledge to herself that she was a really good mother, would it have made it easier for her to accept that her son's behavior was about him, not about her?

When something goes wrong, ask what happened first, don't make snap judgments about yourself or your children. If you are at fault, it's still okay. Change your perception now. There is a reason for your child's behavior. Turn your negative thoughts into positive questions: What part did I play in this situation? Who is my child reminding me of? What can I learn from it? How will correcting this make me a better person? What did I miss that might have changed things? What can I do differently the next time? Don't blame anyone, just find a way to do it differently.

When Portia asked herself who her son reminded her of, the answer was obvious. He looked just like her father, and even had similar facial expressions. Portia had never gotten along with her father; he had always criticized everything she did. Portia needed to stop seeing her father every time Barry got angry or upset. The work she did on that issue improved Portia's relationship with her son.

Make it a habit to ask your children positive questions. If you ask negative questions, their brain and yours will supply negative answers. When you ask positive questions, you will receive positive answers. For example, ask your children, "What do you think you learned from not being prepared for that test? I'm kind of glad that you made this mistake because it will help you to be a better student, and develop work habits that make you proud of yourself. The consequences you experienced must have taught you a lot." This kind of behavior is one of the best lifetime gifts you can give your children.

You didn't think when you got up this morning that this would be the day your life would change, did you? But it's going to happen because the only thing that stands between you and grand success in living are these two things: getting started and never quitting! You can solve your biggest problem by getting started, right here and now.

ROBERT H. SCHULLER
AMERICAN PROTESTANT MINISTER
CRYSTAL CATHEDRAL

Changing Perspective, and Changing Perception

It's never about us as parents. It is always about our children. They have ownership of their life just as we have of ours. Children are full of emotions and feelings. Even young children are indignant if you say no. They know it is their life. They know it is their body. They have ownership.

A five-year-old once told me, "Mommy took away my toy!" You should have heard the astonishment and the indignation in his voice that she dared to do this *to him*. He needed to understand why this happened and what he could do to get his toy back. Since he owned it, he felt his mother had no right to take it away. His mother needed to provide the structure and the rules so he understands his participation in the loss of the toy, and what he needs to do to get it back. It's obvious to us that someone has to be in control, but it's not obvious to our children. Children have to be in control of their bodies, while parents have the greater responsibility of guiding their lives in a positive direction. We have to provide law and order, and give our children the ability to function without disturbing their feelings of self. It's our job to give our children the right to themselves. How do we do that when they bring out our dark side?

It would be magical if each of us could go through life without storing anger, but it usually doesn't happen that way. Our dark side is the anger that we have been storing since childhood, when we didn't have a right to our bodies and to our lives. As children we faced many indignities because our parents didn't know any better. Children are supposed to do what they're told, and parents have to be in control. That was and still is true. But parents can be in charge of the structure they set for children, and still leave them in control of their bodies and their dignity. As parents our dark side is revealed when our children do not listen to us and simply do as they wish.

IMPACT Story: Joanne

Joanne waited for years to become a mother, and she overcame many obstacles to achieve her goal. She had several miscarriages, a serious illness, and finally became pregnant with her first child.

After months of waiting, when Joanne's son, Jonathan, finally arrived on the scene, she vowed to be the best mother ever.

After having a difficult time, Joanne sought therapy. Intuition told her that self-knowledge would be the route to good parenting. Filled with anger, Joanne could not pinpoint its source. She was told that it was normal to feel angry toward her son. Yet at other times, her feelings were too strong, too intense for her to control. When she lashed out at Jonathan, she felt rage and shame for doing so. Joanne asked, "Why am I so angry? He is only three. He couldn't be that bad."

What was smart and solid about Joanne was her willingness to explore her own childhood, so she could discover why she behaved this way. There were other times when she saw herself as the mother she intended to be. At first she denied she had any problems as a child. "My parents were wonderful. They provided a good home for me, took me to the YMCA and Girl Scouts, and did many wonderful things for me. They were good people, and provided a good home. I had a normal childhood."

But when Joanne looked deeper, she remembered one incident that happened when she was a teenager. One day, while having a discussion with her father, she had presented her point of view and felt proud to be able to converse with Dad. She had always thought he was such a bright man. It was a privilege to talk to him on an equal level. But he didn't hear her. He laughed at her carefully thought-out argument, adding insult to injury. She felt dismissed, embarrassed, and ashamed.

It was difficult to remember more incidences. But when she did, they seemed to have the same format. No one ever listened to Joanne. And like all children, she needed to be listened to. Adults had laughed instead, and hadn't taken her seriously. Her parents were always too busy to pay attention to her. Snapshots from her childhood revealed a picture of her rage at her son.

Joanne had told her son to put his toys away three times, but he still didn't listen. When she tried to put him in his high chair, he refused. In fact, she realized that Jonathan rarely listened. She usually overlooked his behavior. But today was different. Other little things went wrong, she forgot to get the mail and blew the deadline on a project she was completing. When her son didn't listen this time, her fuse blew.

• • •

IMPACT in Action

Time out for IMPACT. Let's discover Joanne's childhood pattern, and its effect on her parenting today.

I—I
"I'm bad. I'm always hurting people."

M—My
"My feelings do not count."

P—Perception
Joanne recognized that as a child, she believed that no one ever listened to her. "I'm not important, and what I say doesn't count." Therefore, her perception was that she was not important enough to be listened to.

A—Assumption
Each time Joanne interacted with Jonathan, her underlying assumption was, "Why should he listen to me? I'm not important. I'll just have to keep telling him what to do until he does it. What else can I do? He is my child, and I have to teach him." Because Joanne assumed that Jonathan wouldn't listen, she told him the same thing over and over until he did. Then, afterward, she felt infuriated.

Attitude
Joanne was unaware of the anger and shame she felt when her son didn't listen. Blocked from having a normal response toward him, Joanne was prevented from seeing each situation as it was. Instead, Jonathan continued not to listen as Joanne's rage grew. She felt worthless and unimportant, just as she had felt as a child. Parenting was not turning out to be what she thought it would be. She felt more frustrated than fulfilled.

C—Communication

Joanne had to begin to access her higher self by seeing the best in Jonathan. When she did, she learned she could step out of her surroundings when she began to feel her rage grow. As she took time to breathe deeply, and relax, she could calmly explore the circumstances around her outbursts. It was at those moments that answers appeared.

At first she was ashamed to admit that she lashed out at her three-year-old for not listening. But when she explored the circumstances of her childhood, she remembered that she felt angry and discounted each time her parents didn't listen to her. It became evident that as a parent she was now reliving her own childhood feelings of "not being important enough to be heard, and of feeling discounted most of the time."

T—Trust

As one incident led to the next, Joanne changed her perception by learning to trust herself to explore her childhood feelings, rather than blame herself and feel shame for not being a good mother.

• • •

Joanne began to give herself positive affirmations to take the place of the negative messages that were stuck in her brain, and caused havoc in her present life. This time, when her son didn't listen, she changed her assumption: "My son is not my father. He is my son. He wants to listen to me because I'm important to him. I can teach him how to listen, instead of repeating myself over and over, and getting angry because he doesn't listen."

She adjusted her attitude by reminding herself, "My father was in charge of me then. He would have been better if he knew how. But he wasn't aware that I had feelings, too. I am aware of Jonathan's feelings, and I don't want to ignore them, as my father ignored my feelings. I am in charge now. I can look at why Jonathan doesn't put his toys away when I tell him. If my son is not listening, there must be a reason. Instead of lashing out at Jonathan,

I will uncover my perception, and my assumption, step outside of my circumstances, and communicate with my son. He and I will both benefit."

When Joanne realized where her emotions were coming from, she was able to calmly explore the situation and find a solution. It was different each time, but it sounded like this: "Jonathan is only three. I can help him put his toys away, and feel proud of his accomplishment. I can reward him each time he does what I tell him, so he will develop good feelings from listening to me. The good feelings will replace his indignation at being treated the way I treated him before. I can say, 'Now that you put your Legos in bed with their Lego family, I'm going to read you an extra story tonight because I'm so proud of you for doing such a good job. And Jonathan, you know that you can be proud of yourself too.'"

The nicer Joanne was to Jonathan, the more he listened to her and wanted to please her. Joanne trusted that she would follow through each time she wanted her son to put away his toys, and would eventually do the task himself. The rewards would help him feel confident and make it easier for him to do what was asked. For now, it was Joanne's goal, but as time passed, her son would feel confident enough to follow through with his own goals. Joanne realized that it was worthwhile taking the time to discover where her anger was coming from so she could prevent herself from lashing out at her son, a case of mistaken identity, and unfair to Jonathan.

Although Joanne couldn't always catch her anger in time, her persistence and effort gave her increasingly better results. Both Joanne and her son felt good about building their relationship on understanding and acceptance, rather than on anger. She felt the effort was worth the trouble. What do you think?

Chapter 8

Principle V.
Respect Your Children and They Will Respect Themselves

Whether you want to admit it or not, a lot of your behavior is like your parents—both good and bad. You learned from what you observed them doing, not from what they told you to do. You may be like them or totally opposite, because what they said or did just didn't feel right. If you naturally say "please" and "thank you," your parents may have said that to you. Do you remember hearing "please" and "thank you" from them? How many parents do you know who tell their children to remember their manners, but aren't polite themselves? Which children listen out of respect and which listen out of fear? Is there a difference? What would you like your children to do?

Our children learn from what we do, not from what we tell them to do. When we show them respect, they respect us. Instead of becoming angry, and yelling, hitting, grounding, or punishing, take the time to speak to your children with respect, and explain why you are so upset by what they did. For example, "I am angry because you went to your friend's house without first asking me. When I didn't know where you were, I was worried. I felt much better when you finally called. Thank you for remembering to do that. Then I became angry toward you for not considering me. You know that we have a rule—ask first. I want to know where

you are because I love and care about you. You are very important to me." Then, listen to your child's side of the issue, and
resolve it by saying, "Let's think of a consequence to teach both
of us how to correct this mistake. I must have done something to
give you the impression that it was okay not to ask. What do you
think it should be for each of us?" Most likely there was some
misunderstanding. Give your child the benefit of the doubt.
Knowing that you trust him will make all of the difference.
Discuss what each of you can do to prevent an incident like this
from occurring again. You will be astounded by the ingenuity
your child will have in solving problems, plus his willingness to
make you happy.

You are probably saying, "That's impossible. Are you living in
my house? Sometimes I get so aggravated that I have to walk away
just to stop myself from hitting her. At other times, I can't even do
that." You're right! Whoever said it was easy? Raising children is
the most demanding responsibility we encounter, and you were
right to walk away rather than hit her. Patience, understanding,
and acceptance take time to develop. You might want to look at it
more positively, as your child's way of helping you grow. She's
stretching you, and you will become a better person because of it.

How would you feel if you saw someone yelling at your child,
calling her names, or hitting her, and you watched your child take
it, and not defend herself? What may be difficult to realize is that
you may have treated your child that way at home, and therefore
your child didn't know what else to do. If she wasn't able to defend
herself at home, how will she know how to do it other places?

How many parents do you know who despise the way their
son's wife treats him or their beloved grandchildren, or how their
daughter's husband treats her? Yet, if you had lived in their
house, you would have seen them being treated the same way by
one of their parents. On the other hand, if they had been treated
with respect when they were growing up, they very likely would
have responded differently. Being treated harshly would have felt
wrong, and they wouldn't have been able to tolerate it.

Treat Your Children with Respect

Because Andrea was treated with respect at home she didn't like going to her friend Jane's house. She said, "Mommy, I don't want to go there. Jane's always getting into trouble, and her mother always yells." Andrea knows the difference, and being at Jane's house just doesn't feel good. Can you imagine how relieved Andrea's mother is to know that her child won't allow herself to be in an environment that feels wrong?

When we correct our children, we always need to be specific so they know exactly what we are talking about. When you were little, what did you think when you were sent to your room for talking back. When your parents told you to be nice, did you know what that meant? It seemed to mean something different each time. If you were told that nice meant, "no name-calling, follow directions, ask questions when you don't understand, no screaming, and tell us when you're upset so we can talk about it," you would have had a concrete way to understand the word.

Andrea's friend Jane was only seven. She hasn't been in the world as long as her parents. She still needs words like "nice" explained to her. What do you think would happen if Jane had learned how to express her anger instead of being fresh? She might have said, "Mom, I can't tell you what I'm angry about because that makes you yell at me. If you promise you won't yell, I'll try telling you next time." Wouldn't practicing how to express herself at home, also help her at school and with her friends? Would Andrea have felt more comfortable if Jane's home was like that?

Self-esteem and self-confidence evolve from self-expression. As you gained your parents' praise and approval, your confidence grew. How did you feel when you were able to express feelings, and your parents were proud of you for it, even when you disagreed with them? How did you feel when your parents were able to arrive at a compromise with you? Was it better than screaming and name-calling? How did that help your self-esteem? Did the cycle become self-fulfilling rather than self-defeating, or was the cycle you were in with your parents self-defeating?

As threats of punishment decrease, and confidence in doing the right thing increases, your control and confidence also increase. When your parents begin to understand you for who you are, what you will become and accomplish will be much more than you could have imagined.

Let's look at Tom's situation. His dad went from making fun of Tom to really understanding who he was. At first, his father said, "Why are you such a sissy? You're always reading, reading, reading. When I was your age, I was outside playing all kinds of sports." Was Tom's dad satisfied with who his son was?

But his father finally understood his son's talents when Tom's story appeared in the school newspaper. In fact, he clipped it out, carried it around in his wallet, and showed it to his friends. He asked Tom if he could read other things that he had written. And somehow the message finally came through, "I love you not for what I think you ought to be, but for who you are."

As Tom became older, his father saw how much he loved writing. "I didn't know you thought that way," he said. "Your words are beautiful. You're going to be a writer." That message stayed with Tom. His dad had accepted and approved of who he was. It didn't matter if he became a great writer, or not a writer at all. What mattered was that his father encouraged him to be what he wanted to be; and in his mind, he had the freedom to find out what was in him.

What would have happened if Tom had tried to gain acceptance through athletic ability, because he thought it was the only way to win his father's approval?

Often people attempt to live their lives backwards; they try to have more things, or more money, in order to do more of what they want, so they will be happier.

The way it actually works is the reverse. You must first be who you really are, then do what you need to do, in order to have what you want.

MARGARET YOUNG

Expanding Your Perception

Children come into this world not knowing who they are or what they want to be. Their basic needs are to be fed, sheltered, and nurtured. Newborns cannot differentiate between their mother's face and their face; they reflect back what they see and feel. If the mother's face is smiling and warm, the baby smiles and feels nurtured. If her face is cold and distant, or anxious and impatient, the infant responds in kind. During the first year, babies are too little to differentiate their own feelings from ours. They can only respond to what they are feeling. It is said that our children absorb feelings like a sponge absorbs water.

At about two years, the process of differentiation begins. They begin to realize "I am me, and you are you." They test their limits to further clarify their world, not to defy you. They need to learn about their world through exploration. When we say no, and they say yes, it is not·personal. Their curiosity and intelligence are beginning to develop. When we see their rebelliousness as healthy, we can help them through the exploration stage without damaging their young and often fragile egos.

It's valuable for parents to understand the normal stages of child development. For example, it's normal for a two-year-old to be rebellious; it's crucial for their development. Selma Fraiberg, in her book *The Magic Years*, speaks of the developmental stages children grow through. Don't worry about becoming an expert. All you need to know are some essentials for each stage. You will gain enormous confidence and knowledge knowing what to expect. It's always a good idea to check out a solid book in child development. I recommend books from the Gesell Institute of Childhood Development.

IMPACT Story: Little John

When Little John was two years old, his aunt gave him a shiny new fire engine. He was so focused on the fire engine, and so captivated by its bright color, that he didn't hear his father, Sam, call him. Sam called again, but John kept playing with the toy. So Sam grabbed him, whisked him away from the toy, and hit him hard. "No son of mine will not listen to me."

It might have been helpful if someone had said, "It's not about you, Sam. Your child is only two years old. The toy was captivating for him. What were you afraid of when he disobeyed your command? Why don't you step out of your life long enough to observe that your son is really not out to defy you? He just wants to play with the fire engine your sister gave him. It's his life, not yours. Relax, be there for him, and speak to him with love and kindness. He'll want to listen to you. You're his dad.

"By the time your son is five, his perception of the world will be in place. Will it be one of danger or safety? Picture the type of adult you would like John to become. You, above all, are laying the foundation for him right now. Don't wait until he's grown to decide how you would like him to be. You are programming that person-to-be at this very moment. If you really want to raise an angry and mistrustful adult, you're on the right path. If you want to raise a secure, confident adult, step out of your circumstances, relax, and work to change your perception of the world.

"It's your choice, Sam! You can either reprogram your own perceptions or raise your child to be exactly like you are now—angry and fearful. It's your choice, not his. You're programming the computer. And, he will give back the program you put in place."

Unfortunately, Little John's mother, Denise, wasn't much different. One month later when John was in his high chair eating spaghetti, he squished his tiny hands all over his food feeling its texture, shape, and warmth. He continued exploring as he put it in the palm of his hand and began mussing it all over his face. Unhappily, the slap came, and he was whisked out of his high chair. Denise reprimanded him saying, "No child of mine will eat spaghetti with his fingers."

It would have been helpful to ask Denise, "Who were you seeing, your child or your childhood? Who were you picturing your son to be? Your overweight, slovenly brother? Were you afraid you would feel as ashamed of John as you were of your brother? Why didn't you think he would listen to you by just talking? Do you understand you could hurt him?

"Relax. He is only two. You are his mother. You'll have lots of time to teach him manners when he's old enough to understand. Right now he's appropriately inquisitive. The delicious spaghetti you made for him is new and exciting. Don't destroy his curiosity. It's a precious part of him. This is his life, not yours. Let him begin it with joy and exploration."

Little John grew up to be mistrustful and angry. No one could talk to his parents. They thought they had all the answers. Today, they might feel differently. John the adult prefers his privacy to being with people. If only his parents had been able to step out of their circumstances and understand their son's creative curiosity and great intellect. They missed all of that when they were too busy controlling his every move. Missing out most of all, John promised himself never to have children. He intuitively realized the experience of raising children would bring back painful childhood memories. He could not risk reliving those memories ever again.

Just as the plant has to reach toward the sun to survive, your child has to reach toward his own potential, to follow his or her own instincts, and curiosities. If you place the plant where it cannot get sun, it will twist and turn until it does, or it will die. Does a child react any differently? It's really your child's life, not yours. You're here to encourage his or her emotional well-being; it is not the other way around.

• • •

IMPACT in Action: Little John's Dad

Let's look at Sam, John's father, and how his perceptions affected John.

I—I

"I'm important. My son is going to know that, and he will do what I say, when I say it."

M—My
"My son's feelings do not count as much as mine do."

P—Perception
Sam perceived that Little John was trying to defy him. "My dad never took a role in the family, and I was responsible for everyone. It was too much for me to handle. I hated my childhood. I wanted Dad to be a dad, and he wasn't. I'm not going to be passive like my dad. I'm going to control my family."

A—Assumption
Sam's underlying assumption was, "My son wants to do what he wants, and he doesn't want to listen to me. He's already disrespecting me."

Attitude
Sam needs to change his attitude. John is not living Sam's life. He is trying to live his own life. He doesn't want to control anyone. He is just trying to be a child. He wants to do what any child his age needs to do so he can learn about his world. Sam's life may have been about wanting to have control, and he is putting those feelings onto his son. He needs to give John a chance to be himself, to find out what his life is all about. John is just beginning his own life.

C—Communication
Sam needs to communicate his feelings to John when he doesn't listen. He needs to explain why he feels it is important for John to listen to him. And John will listen, if given a chance. Sam is taking out his anger on his son, anger he felt when his father didn't express his feelings. John needs to experience the world as he encounters it, not as Sam did. John doesn't have to feel angry, guilty, or ashamed just because Sam was when he was little.

Sam can give John the love he wished he had received, and John will return the favor. He will become the confident and secure adult Sam will be proud to have raised. If Sam can respect himself and his feelings, John will grow to respect himself as well.

T—Trust
Sam wanted to respect his father, but his father didn't know how to ask for respect. If Sam asks for respect, he will receive it. He must trust that

John wants to listen to him, and that when he doesn't listen, there is a logical reason. Sam must make an effort to discover the reason. When John is absorbed in either a brand new red truck, or another interest appropriate to his developmental stage, Sam should respect that and give him time to think about and to finish what he's doing before he calls him. Sam can relate differently to John than his father related to him. He can stop the cycle.

• • •

If only Sam could have accessed his higher self, he would have looked for the good side of his son. Then both of their lives could have been quite different.

Chapter 9

Principle VI.
Perfection Isn't the Answer

The paradox of perfection is that the more you try to be perfect, the more imperfect life can be. When you give up the need to be perfect and are able to accept your mistakes, you can do the same for your children. Total acceptance is something each of us strives for and few of us achieve. Yet this is exactly what we need. It allows us to be happy and to grow freely and spontaneously.

Most parents are afraid that if left to their own devices, their children will only want to play. Don't believe it. It isn't true. Didn't you want to do well and to make your parents proud of you? When your inner drive is nurtured, you want to achieve. When you are pushed too hard in any direction, you may react by doing the opposite of what your parents expected.

In all that I read, I had never learned how the search for perfection could have negative consequences. Yet, when I was able to let go of my own need to be perfect, I could also release my children from this bond. Although I never stopped believing in them or in myself, and never stopped encouraging them to do their best, not having to be perfect gave them the space to be who they wanted to be, and the courage to pursue their goals. It put them on a path toward realizing their finest achievements.

I was fortunate to have learned this lesson when they were still young enough to feel the difference. However, my experience has taught me that it is never too late to begin. I adopted the motto, today is the first day of the rest of my life.

If you strive, not for perfection, but for your personal best, your children will emulate you. When you give up perfection, you take the pressure off yourself and your children as well.

Listen and learn from your children. It's an opportunity for your own growth and spontaneity. How good did you feel when your mother listened to you? It might have sounded like this:

> **You:** *Mom, let's play.*
> **Mom:** *Okay, what do you want to play?*
> **You:** *Riddles.*
> **Mom:** *What kind of riddles do you want to do?*
> **You:** *I'll show you. Listen to me.*
> **Mom:** *Okay, go ahead, I never did riddles before. It'll be fun to learn from you.*

Maybe your mother didn't want to play riddles, but she did. Do you think that event would have helped you feel confident and respected? What happened to your feelings about yourself, and your self-esteem? How often did your parents say, "I've got a better game to play. Let's try this one." Maybe their answer was more like "That's no fun. Play with someone else." How did that build your self-esteem?

What if your parent had to win every game? Sally wanted to be silly, and made up silly riddles. When she tried to get her mother to play along, she wouldn't. Her mother was too busy trying to get the answers perfect. Did you have a parent who competed with you? Could that be why you wanted to be silly? It was for Sally. Do you think Sally knew she wouldn't be able to do the riddles as well as her mother? Was her mother aware that she was building herself up, while knocking her daughter down? Why was she doing this? What did Sally remind her mother of? How did her mother's parents treat her?

Did you have a parent who always corrected you for whatever you did, instead of praising you for it? Was your parents' way always better? How did that build your confidence? Do you remember when you showed your homework to Dad, and he said, "That's beautiful, but you left out punctuation." Then Dad showed you how to use periods, commas, semicolons—and especially quotation marks. But your feelings were hurt. All you could remember was what you did wrong, not what your father liked about your work. Then you said, "I'm going to do it my way." How anxious were you to show him another one of your stories? What if you had showed your story to Dad, and he had said, "That's beautiful. I really like it. You're good at writing stories." What would that have done to your confidence? Would you have wanted to write more stories?

Although you may remember what it felt like when you were a child, as a parent you say, "She can't turn in a story without proper punctuation." Why not? Isn't it the teacher's job to teach punctuation? Isn't your job to build confidence and self-esteem? Help your child feel good about herself. How much easier would it have been for you to learn punctuation when you were proud of what you wrote? You do your job as a parent, and let the teachers do theirs. When you try to make your children perfect, their self-esteem will be lowered because at a subconscious and conscious level, they know there's a lot they don't know, and trying to get all that perfect is frightening. Instead, watch for positive and negative influences from situations around you, and help your children realize the difference.

I did that, when I finally learned how to let go of the "perfect" me. So it wasn't perfect, but it did help, and it balanced the critical side of my husband. Although Eddie changed later on, our children are the ones who have the real challenge. It's their turn now. If they work on letting go of perfection, while still doing their best, then their children will benefit.

When your children are little, they're eager to learn from you. Take advantage of that time you have with them. When they're older, they'll want to learn on their own. Let's hope their eagerness doesn't diminish as their age increases. Look around you. Do you see that happening a lot?

Quit Finding Faults in Your Children

It doesn't work. It erodes self-confidence. Do you remember when you were five, and wanted Mom to play with you? She said, "I'm too busy doing housework now." You might have answered, "Mommy, can I help you make the beds so you can have time to play with me?" "Of course, that's a good idea." You proudly made your bed and ran to tell Mom, and she said, "That's good, but you have to tuck in the corners, and smooth the spread more even over the entire bed." Even if you were disappointed at her response, you might have tried again. What if she said, "That's much better. Thank you." But right before you went outside, Mom went over your work, making the bed more perfect than you could ever do at five. How do you think you would have felt? You might have thought, "Whatever I do, it's just not good enough. I wish I were perfect like Mom. I'll never get it the way she wants it." After that, did Mom understand why you wouldn't make the bed again, or do other things when she asked?

When you tell your children by your actions or your words what they're doing wrong, they begin to say that to themselves. When you're critical of your children, they become critical of themselves. When they become adults, what you've said to them remains "alive in their subconscious" for them to say to themselves.

Now, if your mother had been proud of your work, and left it alone, how would you have felt about yourself that day? That feeling would have carried over into other things you did. Would you have tried harder each time Mom praised you? Would that have helped you feel confident about doing other things for your mother, and eventually for yourself?

What kind of words do you say to yourself now that you're an adult? Many people tell themselves they can't do anything right. They've absorbed the messages they heard so often as a child. Now when others tell them, "You can do it. You're so talented. Look what you've accomplished already. Keep at it. I know you can do it," they don't take it in. Their inside voice is louder saying, "No I can't. I never get it right."

Find things your children do right. So they get color on the kitchen counter again. So what? The counter can be cleaned, and it is going to be there a lot longer than your children will be children. Praise their drawings and they'll be glad to clean up their crayon marks. Watch fear fly away, and confidence fly in.

> *We are not in a position in which we have nothing to work with. We already have a start; we already have capacities, talents, direction, missions, callings.*

> *The job is, if we are willing to take it seriously, to help ourselves to be more perfectly what we are, to be more full, more actualizing, more realizing, in fact, what we are in potentiality.*

> ABRAHAM MASLOW
> AMERICAN PSYCHOLOGIST
> (A FOUNDER OF HUMANIST PSYCHOLOGY)

Why Isn't Perfection the Answer?

Nature isn't perfect. There is the beauty of the mountains, oceans, sunrises, sunsets, but there is also the destruction of tornadoes, hail, snowstorms, floods, volcanoes, and fires. To every front there is a back, to every top there is a bottom. And so perfection has a downside as well.

When raising our children, we want them to be perfect, to be everything we couldn't be. In addition, we want them to have all that we didn't have. We look at these precious little beings and we want the world to love them as much as we do. Although we've never had children before, we expect to have the most perfect painting—a masterpiece, all without any formal training.

What a setup! How many people do you know who can read a book without having been taught how to read? There are a few geniuses in the world, but not many. Yet, isn't perfection what we expect of our children? Somehow we believe if we keep telling our children what they did wrong they will become the perfect people we want them to be.

The irony is that the more perfect we raise our children to be, the more imperfect they become. We seem to focus on what the eye can see: the way they look, dress, or talk, their manners, the way they clean their room, read, write, do their homework.

We actually believe the more we tell our children what to do, when to do it, and how to do it, the more perfect they will become. Unfortunately, learning is not that simple. It is, however, challenging, demanding, and often paradoxical. The more we tell our children to do it "our way," the more they will do it "their way." Because in the process of raising our children, we forget to focus on what is most important to them—their feelings.

Our children are like diamonds. They have the potential to be as beautiful on the inside as they are on the outside. What if a diamond cutter was so intent on cleaning, sanding, and shining the outside of each diamond that he forgot to handle it carefully enough, and destroyed the natural beauty of its individual facets? Yet, the more facets that shine through, the more beautiful and valuable the diamond is.

I meet so many people who appear to be perfect on the outside. They look, dress, and speak magnificently; and their homes are masterpieces as well. They are so attractive they could adorn the cover of a fashion magazine. But their insides are badly damaged. Their parents, in the quest for perfection, somehow forgot to pay attention to the feelings of their children. A model will talk about how fat he is, a famous writer of what's wrong with her work, an executive of fearing failure each time she steps into her office. A woman who stays at home to raise her children feels worthless because she doesn't have a career, and society doesn't value her choice of work—even though she does, although she doesn't have the confidence to speak of it.

If we do not believe in ourselves, how can we believe in our children? If we haven't been able to appreciate our own qualities, how can we appreciate those of our children?

As parents striving for perfection, we usually focus on our children's homework, grades, performance in sports, Scouts, religious instruction, and so on. All of these activities are of value, and help to build competence and self-esteem. But if our children are criticized for not being good enough, doesn't that defeat the purpose of all that instruction? Isn't it important for us to focus on our children's thoughts and feelings regarding their numerous activities and daily challenges? Do we find time for that? Did your parents pay attention to your inner needs and desires?

In today's world our children have schedules as filled as ours. When are they children, with time to relax, time to talk, time to play? When I ask children this question, the response is usually, "I play on Saturday." Some children are lucky enough to play with their friends two days a week. Is there something wrong with this picture? How are we helping our children to perfect their inner selves, their feelings, what they want, and who and what they will become?

When is there time for families to be together as families? Thank goodness for the Fourth of July, Thanksgiving, Hanukkah, Christmas, church or synagogue or mosque. But what about the rest of the year? When you add in the staggering divorce rate, do you wonder what is happening to our children today?

Many highly successful people I meet are always busy. When they stop running, they face emptiness. They're not happy and don't understand why. They have accumulated all the material goods, but at the end of the day, that simply isn't enough.

The ingredients of true happiness—inner peace, inner knowing, and inner security—may be eluding them. Few of us realize that we begin to find true happiness when we know and understand our children. Seeing the world through our children's eyes helps us to relive our own childhood, to see the world in a new and special way.

When we begin to know and understand ourselves, we can then begin to fill the emptiness inside. Just imagine how many happy children we are likely to create. If we wait to discover our own happiness, and who we really are, will it be too late for our children to reap the benefits? What models have we provided for them? How can we help our children develop their inner selves, their happiness, when we haven't done it for ourselves? When we discover our inner feelings, our outer presence will not need to be perfect. We will be who we are meant to be, and we will be on the road toward peace of mind and contentment.

IMPACT Story: Rita

Rita's mother was an incredibly beautiful woman. She was a blur of activity, always fixing, making ceramic pottery, doing, doing, everything had to be perfect. There was no time for Rita. Her father would wait for her mother at the bottom of the steps on a Saturday night beaming from top to bottom. She was passionate, and had many friends. But when she became angry at her friends, they were exiled from her life.

Rita never felt valued. "Nobody ever heard me. I had to do what Mom told me to do. She taught me to trust people—not to hold their lack of education against them. I was so scared of her. I was too scared to tell her about how my husband, John, abused me, because I thought she would blame me for it. I knew God was bigger than I was, but I didn't know where God was or where to look for him. I didn't know if he really heard. Mom should have saved me from John."

Rita's mother was unpredictable. She often hit her daughter. "She shouldn't have made me bleed, or called me a liar. Mom shouldn't have been so unpredictable. She should have shared the important things that were going on with me, so I would understand. I was always in the dark until I was practically grown up."

Rita admired her mother, and wanted to be like her in so many ways. "I think I provoked Mom when I was most like her. She saw something in me that scared her, but she never explained her feelings to me. I felt she saw something in me that was bad, then she would try to beat it out of me. Mom made me believe I was bad, but I never knew why.

"I loved her passionately. She was the center of my life. There didn't seem to be anything she couldn't do. People wanted to be around her. They loved her even though there were so many times she was so sad. It was because she had had a terrible child-hood, and had grown up in poverty. She had had a sick father who tried to beat her. Mom must have been very wild because she used to see that in me."

Rita developed a deep need for consistency, a deep need to know, and not to be kept in the dark. But she married to a man who keeps her in the dark and doesn't follow through with what he says he will do. "It is so painful to be with him, but I love him, just as I loved Mom. When he lies to me, I feel helpless, just as I felt as a child. Yet, I love him, and I allow him to treat me badly. I don't know any other way. I feel like a child when I'm around him, and I can't take myself out of the situation."

● ● ●

IMPACT in Action: Rita

I—I
"I'm not important."

M—My
"My feelings don't count. No one hears me."

P—Perception
Rita believed that other people were more important than her. "I have to please them so they will like me. If I don't, I feel worthless."

A—Assumption
She assumed that she was supposed to be treated badly because she was bad. "Mom made me believe that about myself. When I'm treated badly, I feel like a child, helpless. I feel as if I don't deserve to be loved, or treated well." Rita continued the behavior with her children. " There are times that I'm mean to my children, and I berate them mercilessly, but I can't stop myself. At these times, I know I am like my mother."

Attitude

Rita needs to change her attitude. She needs to believe that she is worthwhile and deserves happiness. "I don't want to be depressed like Mom, and I don't want to treat my children badly." Rita can begin to access her higher self by seeing her best self and saying, "I am good, I am not bad. I deserve love." She needs to repeat this affirmation until she feels confident inside. When that happens she will react differently toward her husband.

C—Communication

Rita needs to communicate to her husband, to stand up to him when he speaks cruelly, to no longer take his abuse. Either they both change, or she leaves the marriage. "I cannot afford to be afraid of him anymore. It is more painful to stay in this abusive situation than to break through my fears and leave it."

T—Trust

Finally, Rita must trust herself to treat her children differently. She has to ask for their help in telling her when she's mean to them, as her mother was to her. "I know when I change the way I am to my children, I will no longer allow the insults from my husband. I will speak nicely to him, even when he treats me badly. I don't want to do to him what he does to me. I know that standing up for myself will encourage me to leave him, unless he changes the way he relates to me."

• • •

∾ Chapter 10 ∾

Principle VII.
Never Do for Your Children What They Can Do for Themselves

Helping your children do things for themselves is what gives them confidence. When do you feel most confident? Are you happier when you are really good at something or when someone else does it for you? Do you choose your own clothes each morning? Of course you do. You probably wouldn't have it any other way. Then how do you think your children feel when you choose their clothes for them each morning? How would that make you feel? How would you learn what you want to wear if you had no experience deciding? So what if you dress perfectly?

Allow Your Child to Experience Consequences

Do you brush your children's teeth for them? Whose teeth are they anyway? What about a special reward for no cavities, instead? I'd rather give some money to my children than much more to the dentist. I tried this tactic, and it worked. Each checkup was better than the one before. My boys had developed good habits and lots of confidence from being responsible for their teeth.

What if your children don't brush their teeth correctly and get cavities? How fast will they learn when they realize their part in this? Won't the filling be a natural consequence? Do you think they'll learn from experience when they are given the opportunity? What if you brush their teeth, and they still get cavities?

Each new task you mastered as a child was another step toward self-confidence. Isn't it the same for your children? When your children are small they develop confidence from handling their body. They progress from crawling to walking to toilet-training to dressing themselves. Never do for them what they can do for themselves. Help them help themselves. When they ask for help, guide them instead. The more your children do for themselves, the more they naturally improve. The more your children are praised for what they do, the more they'll want to do, and the more confident they will be.

How did Marcos react when his mother took responsibility for his homework? "Marcos, you have to do your homework! Where is your algebra book? Why did you leave it at school again?" Marcos's actions and words told her that he didn't want her to be in charge of his homework. His mother just didn't hear him. When she wouldn't let up, he left his books at school. He finally stopped doing his homework, and failed his algebra test.

Whose homework was it? Marcos's mother cared more about his homework, and suffered more from his failure, than he did. Marcos knew it. He expressed his anger in actions, rather than words. The more she became involved, the less work Marcos did. And the less Marcos did, the less capable he felt he was. "Why doesn't she get it?" he'd ask himself. "I'm almost thirteen and she's still doing my homework. She makes me feel as if I can't do anything without her. Sometimes I think she's right."

If his mother had really listened to him, Marcos would have felt differently; because she didn't, he felt he wasn't worth being listened to. Can you see why Marcos developed low feelings of self-esteem and self-worth? But doesn't a parent have to step in if a child isn't doing homework? Of course.

What did your parents do? If you knew your parents respected and trusted you, and if you were having a problem doing your homework, could you ask them to help you? Would you have skipped your homework knowing your parents had confidence that you would ask for help, and work through your problems? If you knew that your parents respected you enough to handle the consequences, would you respect yourself? Wouldn't experiencing consequences also help you realize that it's up to you to change the results?

Now, Marcos is angry because his mother tries to do everything for him. He sabotages himself by thinking, "I'd rather not do anything than have Mom tell me what to do all the time." His mother's job is to be there for Marcos. His job is to be there for himself. The situation is reversed. By not allowing Marcos to be there for himself, he doesn't really know how to be there. He's reacting out of anger, not out of respect for himself.

By responding to and respecting what your children say and do, you show them respect and trust. It helps them feel important and develop self-esteem. When you trust your children, you show it. They feel that trust—and they won't let you down. When you really hear your children, you'll know how to help them rather than hurt them. Were you really heard?

When We Don't Listen

There are times when our children's biggest problem is us. How does your child tell you when she has a problem with you? What if your child feels that you give his brother or sister more attention? What if she just thinks you're unfair?

When our children feel this way, they may either tell us or they may be afraid to reveal these feelings. Perhaps they cannot articulate them adequately, or they're not aware of how they feel. For good reason, children may believe we'll say, "Dearest, it just isn't true! I love you as much as I love your brother, or sister. Don't feel this way." But if your child does feel "this way," there is a reason.

We treat each one of our children differently. And we may not be aware of our tone of voice, facial expression, body language, or when or why we do this. If we can acknowledge that it may be possible to be partial to one of our children, we then can begin to ask ourselves why this may be true, and what we can do to change. Very few parents wish to be partial, they just don't know any better, but it can be devastating to a child. What was it like for you?

Accept that it is okay to have human frailties, and try to find out why you are reacting in the way you are. Isn't acknowledging your child's feelings a better alternative than not believing her, thus causing her to doubt her reality and her thought processes?

When children are not listened to, or believed, they may choose one of five or more roles to play in order to get their needs met. They either become the star, the rebel, the adaptive child who does everything just to please you, the scapegoat (or victim), or the quiet one who watches from the sidelines. Adopting any of these roles prevents your child from discovering who he is, and what he wants to be.

Go confidently in the direction of your dreams!
Live the life you've imagined.
As you simplify your life,
the laws of the universe will be simpler;
solitude will not be solitude,
poverty will not be poverty,
nor weakness weakness.

HENRY DAVID THOREAU
AMERICAN WRITER (1817–1862)

IMPACT Story: Charlie

Charlie was five years younger than his brother, Chet. He wanted Chet to love him more than anything. Charlie wanted to be just like Chet. But Chet didn't feel the same way at all. Once Charlie arrived on the scene, Chet's life changed drastically. Charlie was sick a lot; he even had to be rushed to the hospital several times. He cried a lot, and always got his parents' attention.

Chet wanted things to be the way they were before Charlie arrived; but he knew that wasn't possible. So he did the only thing he could do at the time. Chet made an unconscious decision to please Mom and Dad and therefore receive much needed attention. Each time Chet took care of his younger brother, he resented him even more. He was mean to Charlie. Chet acted like the perfect child in front of his parents. He didn't tell them his real feelings. When Charlie complained that Chet was mean to him, his parents believed Chet. So Chet continued to be nasty to his little brother. Whenever Chet complained to Mom and Dad that Charlie didn't listen to him, Charlie got into trouble. His parents didn't believe him. So Charlie thought they loved his older brother more than him. "Chet acts so perfect. He always does what Mom and Dad want him to do. They don't see how mean he is to me, and worse than that they don't ever believe me."

Charlie became the family scapegoat. Whenever Mom and Dad called family meetings to talk about family problems, Charlie was blamed. Charlie hated talking. No matter what he said, it was always his fault. Charlie cried each time he was left with Chet. After a while, it became too unpleasant for Mom and Dad to leave. The problem continued to get worse.

If only these parents hadn't taken sides. If they had believed both boys, they would have recognized that Charlie and Chet were not communicating their real feelings. Instead of taking sides, they could have been there to support each child in expressing his feelings. They could have helped Charlie say what he meant by listening very carefully, and giving him words to express his feelings, not by doing it for him.

• • •

IMPACT in Action: Chet

I—I
"I don't count anymore. Charlie gets all the attention."

M—My
"My life isn't the same since my brother came."

P—Perception
Chet believes that it's Charlie's fault that he doesn't get attention. He thinks that everything would be okay if only Charlie weren't around. "I hate him, but I'm afraid to tell Mom and Dad what I really feel."

A—Assumption
Chet assumes that if he tells his parents how he really feels, they won't love him. "Mom and Dad love my brother more than me."

Attitude
Chet hates his brother. "If it wasn't for him, I'd be happy."

C—Communication
Mom and Dad could have encouraged Chet to express his feelings, good and bad. They may have said, "Feelings aren't bad, they are just feelings. When we talk about them, they lose their power. We know it is difficult to tell your younger brother how you feel. Tell us, and we'll help you express your feelings to him. We'll also help Charlie understand what you say. Is it okay if we help him talk to you too?"

T—Trust
When Chet learns to express his feelings, he will be able to express them to his friends and teachers, and in other areas of his life. Chet will benefit as will the rest of the family. Isn't it amazing how families create problems for themselves? Chances are either or both of Chet's parents had been the favorite in their respective homes, and one of their siblings had also been the unfortunate scapegoat.

Won't the whole family benefit when they each learn how to express their feelings, and not disbelieve or blame the other?

• • •

Chapter 11

Principle VIII.
Eliminate Blame from Your Vocabulary

If you think you've made a mistake, focus on accepting that it happened for a reason. Then give yourself time to find it, correct it, learn from it, and let it go. Have confidence that you'll do better the next time.

Or are you one of the many people who go over and over your mistakes? If you could have done it differently, you would have. You just didn't know any other way. Forget "should have," "would have," or "could have"—they are the most nonproductive, destructive words in the English language. Instead, begin each day by saying, "What can I do differently, so that what happened won't happen again?" Then do it. In other words, let go of blame, and correct the problem. Try spending 90 percent of your time on the solution, and 10 percent of your time on the problem. You'll be amazed at the results.

Children Are Literal Thinkers

Keep in mind that children are literal. They believe exactly what you say about them. What did you think when your dad said, "You're supposed to be smart, why do you do such stupid things?" Could it have been, "He really means I'm stupid. I guess I am."

Then your mother said, "Can't you hear? How many times do I have to tell you not to slam the door?" You probably really thought something was wrong with you. "Dad thinks I'm stupid, and I don't even hear Mom."

There is a very good chance that your child will interpret your off-hand remarks literally. So why not make them positive? How would you feel if your child's teacher spoke to your child that way?

Try saying, "Knowing how smart you are, I'm certain you didn't take the time to think about what you just did. I know you'll do better the next time." And if your child didn't hear you, you might say, "When I tell you something and you don't hear it, you must be thinking about something else. What would you like me to do to get your attention so you'll hear what I've said?" How would that make your child feel?

> *There is one thing stronger than all the armies of the world, and that is an idea whose time has come.*
>
> VICTOR HUGO
> FRENCH AUTHOR (1802–1885)

IMPACT Story: Edythe

Not until our children are born do we realize how profound an experience it is. We find ourselves responsible for little people before we have truly grown up and fully understood ourselves. At least, that was the case for me.

Before our twins arrived on the scene, I was still a child. There was no one else that I was responsible for. I was married, but my husband was responsible for himself and his career. I was responsible for myself and my career. As we worked together, and supported each other in our endeavors, we had little to worry about, except having enough money to eat, having a roof over our heads, and enjoying life. Beyond that we were relatively free to do what we wanted, and to help each other in ways that we each needed.

I thought my husband was rather critical of me. I wasn't aware that I was also critical of my children until the day their nursery school teacher said, "You're children are so wonderful, and smart. I really enjoy having them in my classroom." I replied, "They're not that good. There's a lot of things they do wrong." And she said, "They're only children. They're supposed to make mistakes. Why don't you focus on all of the good things they do, and enjoy them?"

Suddenly I realized a part of me was negative when that part focused on what they did wrong. I wasn't consciously aware of what I, too, was doing until a remark from a professional, and an expert in working with children, forced me to stop and listen.

When I thought about it, I realized that both my husband's family and my own rarely remarked about how adorable our children were. They either pointed out the mistakes we were making with the twins, or what was wrong with the boys. As a result, we both found ourselves being defensive when we were with our families. Neither one of us realized that we were raising our children the way our parents had raised us. It was unconscious on our part, as I later learned it is for almost every parent.

I hadn't even been aware that my husband was a blamer until our children arrived, and my husband and I shared parenting. The reality is that our backgrounds, and the way we were raised, had a powerful impact on our lives. We had the same "blaming" wounds from childhood, but we were each parented very differently. Also, we handled our wounds in the opposite way, as I later learned most couples do. He blamed me, and I blamed myself.

I now know we're not unique; it wasn't happening just to us—it happens to all of us. We marry people who have backgrounds that are very opposite to ours, but who have similar childhood wounds. We are not aware that our unconscious has chosen our mate so we could work through our childhood wounds with him or her.

When we were children, we were helpless in the way we were raised. When we became adults, we weren't aware that we could change this pattern, change our perceptions, undo our childhood pain, and be free of the wounding patterns. The person we married may have appeared to be different from our mother or father, but after being married a few years, we begin to realize he or she has the same negative and positive traits of our parents. (If you are interested in learning more, read *Getting the Love You Want* by Harville Hendrix.)

It was no accident that my husband was like my family, critical and uninvolved like my father. He kept telling me what to do, but didn't do it himself. I was unaware of his reactions to me because they were so familiar. My family had always reacted to me that way. How could I know that other people react differently, or that it wasn't always my fault? How could I know I was unconsciously attracted to my husband because he was like my parents? If I had known, I wouldn't have married him. Even though I loved my parents, I never expected to repeat their mistakes with my family.

When we co-parent, we want to do the very best we can for our children. When we become parents, most of us do not wish to repeat the negative patterns of our parents. Unfortunately, most of what happened to us in childhood is buried deeply in our subconscious minds. We do not repeat what we consciously remember, but we do repeat what is in our subconscious childhood history. And often we unintentionally do to our children what was done to us. We unconsciously repeat what happened to us when we were children at the same age of our children.

Before our children came into the world, my husband and I enjoyed each other and our lives together. If my husband blamed me for making a mistake, I wasn't really aware of it because I was in the habit of blaming myself.

My husband wasn't aware he was doing to me what had been done to him in his childhood. He was blamed for everything, so he naturally followed that pattern, and blamed me for everything. I didn't know any better because when I was a child, my family blamed me, and I blamed myself. We were a perfect match: each handling our childhood wound in the opposite way, each coming from a family whose mode of operation was "blaming." The pattern intensified when we had two children at once. The blaming became so difficult for me to absorb that I was forced to notice it.

As my children grew older, and I realized that they had some responsibility in their lives, I took my first grown-up step. I couldn't allow the "blaming" pattern to continue. It was devastating to me, and to the children; and at that time, my husband just didn't know any better. I was equally at fault for accepting all of the blame, as if the world would not continue without me being responsible for everything. Then, I realized I had to teach my children how to take care of themselves because it was beyond my power to do it all. I also knew "blaming" had to go out of our lives—forever! There was just no room for it in our family.

But before I could fix us, I had to fix me. That meant that I had to stop blaming myself. I also had to become aware of when I was critical, even though I thought I wasn't. It was a difficult process. When I changed my behavior, it became obvious to my husband that he too had to change his behavior. The old ways were no longer working for either of us. Change had to happen soon. We decided to work on learning what we could do since it would have been more painful to divorce. We pooled our resources, and separately and together, we stretched and grew into a new marriage. My husband demonstrated that he loved us enough to work on himself, and to change the family patterns he contributed to our marriage. We had to change, and we did. And everyone benefited.

It happened in our family; it can happen in yours. It took fortitude and courage to change, but it was worth the effort. As a marriage and family counselor, I see the consequences of divorce are much more severe than the necessary tools needed to grow into a more fully realized family. I tell my clients, "When you change the way you behave toward the other person, he will do the thing he does more. When it no longer works, the other person will change the way he is toward you. If he won't change, and insists on staying with damaging behavior, only then will it be time to look at the possibility of ending the relationship."

We each are responsible for changing ourselves, although most of us insist that the other is the one who needs the changing. Today it is fairly accurate to state that, with notable exceptions, we have not learned how to love. If we had, more than one out of two marriages wouldn't end in divorce. And how many people are in unhappy marriages?

Our parents, and their parents, went through hard times—two world wars, and the Great Depression. Our parents were concerned with survival. They didn't have the luxury of focusing on being happy. Our generation is involved in an equally devastating war. It is very personal; our families are being destroyed. It is time for us to learn how to love, so we do not continue damaging our children and destroying our families. Imagine for a moment how different married life would have been if our folks had focused on seeing themselves and their children in a more positive light? If they had focused on what we did right rather than on what we did wrong? Determined to create a happy, loving family, I was the one who set out to change our old patterns. In other words, I was in more pain than my husband. The patterns didn't bother him enough. He simply accepted what was. It happens that way in most marriages. One partner is called the dragee, while the other is the drager. The dragee won't settle for less than happiness and the solid change required to do what it takes to achieve it. The other partner usually goes along. Of course, there are other ways of not settling such as overwork, substance abuse, divorce, insanity, and even murder.

I like the option we chose, although it isn't for everyone. Nothing can be perfect, but we can truthfully claim to have accomplished a positive, powerful change within our family. You can do it too.

Life is a continual pattern of growth and change, just as we see in nature—flowers bloom in the spring and die in the winter. Marriages also have seasons, and developmental stages. As my husband and I changed the old patterns, we demonstrated to our children that they will not have to settle for an unhappy marriage either. When their turn comes, as it generally does for most of us, they will have the tools for understanding what to do, and the knowledge that change is possible and worth beginning.

• • •

IMPACT in Action: Edythe

Let's look at how my husband's blaming response impacted our children and my feelings toward him; and the first steps I took to change myself, and my patterns.

I—I
"I knew I counted, but I didn't know how."

M—My
"My feelings were hurt each time I was blamed for what my children did."

P—Perception
When my husband said, "Eydie, watch the baby, he's going to fall," I perceived myself as incompetent, and worried that I didn't love my sons enough to protect them.

A—Assumption
My assumption was that my husband thought I was incompetent and selfish.

Attitude
This assumption affected my attitude, and blocked my positive feelings toward my husband. I felt angry, and wanted to lash out at him because I assumed he didn't trust me as a parent, and thought I was selfish and incompetent.

When I stepped out of the circumstances, and visualized my childhood, I realized I was reacting to my husband from the way I was treated as a child. I remembered being called "selfish" whenever I didn't do what my parents wanted. I often felt frustrated because I knew deep down that I wasn't selfish. Usually parental perceptions have far more power over the child than her differing belief of herself.

A turning point in my life occurred when I enrolled in college. Even though I paid my own tuition, my parents considered it selfish. The reality was that my parents had different priorities than I had. It wasn't personal. They just hadn't separated me from them, and they were projecting their financial insecurities and fears onto me. It was a case of mistaken identity. They wanted me to work and save money, rather than postpone the financial rewards that college would bring later in my life. Were they being selfish, or were they unaware of greater possibilities? Their own fears blocked them from being there for me in the way I needed them to be. As a teenager, their priorities didn't make sense to me. I thought they didn't love me—and it hurt. I felt selfish going to college, even though I didn't think the other college students I saw were selfish. I was reacting to the perception my parents had of me, and that's what had to change.

When I married and had children, I made a conscious decision not to be selfish. But I still needed to change my assumption. My husband had to know that I wasn't selfish. I realized how important it was to communicate this feeling to him, because it affected our marriage, and our children. It wasn't easy to change my assumption. I had to gain access to my higher self, and have it help me see the honest, true part of me— not what my parents saw. I told myself at least one hundred times every day, "I am not selfish. I am a very good mother and wife. I love and care about my family more than anything in the world. I will not allow anyone to call me selfish again. It simply is not true." Changing my assumption helped change my attitude. When I did, the feelings I originally had toward my husband gradually began to return. *I promised me that when he made a comment that didn't feel right, I would take the higher path, and change the meaning I took from his comment.* Instead I would say to myself, "What does that have to do with me? He is trying to help; he is not implying that I am selfish. I can tell him how sensitive I am to his choice of words later, when this has passed. I know he will consider my feelings after that. If he doesn't I will remind him again. My feelings count, and so do his."

C—Communication

Now I decided that if he didn't "get it" because I don't "communicate it," nothing will change. Therefore, I made a second commitment to myself: to communicate my feelings to him, and to be sure he understood them. That meant I planned to follow through with either a thank you when he made a conscious communication change toward me, or to find another time to explain the feeling I had if he did call me selfish again.

It wasn't easy! There were many instances when I felt upset, or angry. And when I went back to my childhood to discover why I felt the way I did, the reason was waiting for me to find. I knew it was best to work on one circumstance at a time.

You might wonder what this has to do with parenting. The answer is that it has everything to do with how we parent. The anger we feel at our spouse or children is generally about us, and the perceptions, assumptions, and attitudes we acquired from childhood. When we have unexpressed anger toward our spouse, it affects our interactions with our children. Even when all goes well with our spouse and work-related situations, if we have anger toward our children, it is still usually about our childhood.

Stepping out of these perceptions, assumptions, and circumstances enables us to be mature adults with our children. We can react to them by understanding we have a message to teach, rather than engaging in a power struggle.

T—Trust
My next step was to trust myself that I would communicate, rather than allow my husband's remarks to hurt our family. I would work on my own feelings, until I responded differently to his comments, and would concentrate on not allowing myself to feel "selfish" or to be called selfish.

I encouraged the boys to express their feelings to us. When I noticed any negative comments from my husband toward the children, we would talk about it. When either of them noticed any negativity coming from me, they promised to talk about it.

● ● ●

The more we did—together and separately—changed our family's emotional environment, and I believe the future environment of our children and grandchildren as well. I watch my sons as positive adults, praising each other when they can, being supportive, and being there for each other and themselves by constructively challenging derogatory circumstances in their lives.

Most important, I have made a commitment to myself that I will not live in unhappy circumstances. I will do what I have to in order to take care of my feelings, and my happiness, and to access and live within my higher self. Just as the seasons change and new growth appears, I will continually change and grow. If I find myself stuck, I pray that I will do what it takes to leave that place behind me.

Chapter 12

Principle IX.
Say No to Negativity

No matter what happens, find a way to see the positive side of a situation. This habit will help you survive happily. As you know, things happen in cycles. There will be bad times and good times. Wouldn't you be a lot happier if you knew how to find what's good, even in the bad times?

Do you find yourself saying, "Everything always happens to me. Isn't this ever going to stop?" If you really think about it, everyone has problems; it's part of life. If you focus on the good things as well, you might find many good things happen to you too.

Make Every Challenge an Opportunity

Maybe the bad is there to teach you. I can hear you say, "No thanks, I've had enough lessons." That may be true, but if you realize that there's something good to learn from everyone, life can be a lot more pleasant. In truth, good and bad situations happen to everyone, just some get more than others. Maybe some of us have more to learn. Many of us don't deserve what happens to us. We can't always help what happens, but we can help the way we view it. For example, you could take the approach, "I've had a lot of good things happen recently, so when the bad started I was ready for it. After all, I know that the good won't last forever. Everything runs in cycles, so I'll ride these waves until the cycle turns." Isn't that a more pleasant way to go through life? The way you handle the bad will stretch and grow you to be a happier, better person. Practice seeing the glass as half full rather than as half empty and keep your mind focused on what you can do rather than on what you can't do.

When your child says, "I can't do this math homework, it's just too hard," help him develop a new way of thinking about it. At his age, homework is a serious problem. You think your problems are a lot worse. What's important is how you have learned to handle them. Why not break the problem down into smaller steps, and praise yourself and your children for each step along the way. Remembering to never do for your child what he can do for himself, you can say, "Let's have a look at it. What part is confusing for you?" When he still says he can't do it, try taking a break and looking at it again later. Tell him, "I'm sure you can do it. You just need some time to think about it." Then, of course, Principle XI, "Follow Through," will apply. (See Chapter 14.)

When you believe there is always a way to find a solution, your child will also. When you believe "can't" is a bad word, your child will too. Is the glass half empty or half full?

Coping with Divorce: Tom's Story

Let's look at how Tom viewed the world since his parents divorced. "First Dad left Mom, then he moved far away, then he married, and had three more children. He says he loves me, but I don't believe him. If he did, why would he do all of these things without thinking of me?" Tom has a point. It does seem as if his world is falling apart and that he is fifth in his father's eyes. What would you say to him?

Tom's mother held up a glass half-filled with water and asked, "Is this glass half empty or half full?" Tom answered without hesitation, "Half empty." She said, "Tom, you're seeing all of the bad, and not much of the good; kind of like Eeyore in

Winnie-the-Pooh. Let's pretend for a minute that you were like Pooh, what good would you see that Dad does?" Tom thought and thought, "He calls me, he takes me places, and I have fun when I visit him. I get to visit a new state and learn new things about the world."

When she asked him which way of looking at his life made him happier, he replied the second way, but he was afraid to do that. "How do I know what else Daddy will do?" "Time will tell," she told him, "We'll see. Life has both good and bad parts. Let's take time to enjoy the good for now. If Dad doesn't keep his promises, you will learn how important promises are, and when you grow up, you'll remember to keep promises to your children. If Dad keeps his promises, you can see the good that came out of that bad." Tom said, "I think I'm going to try to be like Pooh. I'll wait and see."

Mom said, "I feel better looking at the good as well as the bad, do you?" He answered, "Yep, seeing the bright side helps."

The greater the contrast, the greater the potential.

Great energy only comes from a correspondingly
great tension between opposites.

CARL GUSTAV JUNG
SWISS PSYCHOLOGIST AND PSYCHIATRIST (1875–1961)

Adjusting Your Attitude

Can you step outside of your circumstances and adjust your attitude so you can see the positive, rather than the negative, aspect of a situation? The first question you may want to ask is, "Do I really want to see the bright side of life? Or would I rather expect the bad, and protect myself from being hurt by believing differently?"

As President Franklin Roosevelt once said, "The only thing we have to fear is fear itself." Is it fear that stops you? Most people would rather stay with what they know than reach out for the unknown; they fear what they don't know and they fear losing what they have. Other people would say, "Nothing ventured, nothing gained." Of course the first statement is the dark side while the second statement represents the bright side. You make the decision. Which path would you like to take as you go through life?

You probably have also heard, "Watch out what you ask for, because you just might get it." Asking is the first step, having your actions match your words is the second. Many people ask for what they want, but their actions do not match. Most of us get exactly what we ask for through our actions and words. We can decide to learn great lessons from the bad things that come our way, or we can feel sorry for ourselves, and not learn anything. It's our choice.

IMPACT Story: Julie

Julie, the second youngest of twelve children, was so good. All she ever wanted was to be loved. But her mother had little money, and eleven other children to feed and clothe. So Julie received love by watching her mom. She watched her cook, clean, and take care of each of the children. By the time it was Julie's turn, her mother was too exhausted to read her a story, or even talk to her. It didn't happen because it couldn't happen. Julie's mother just couldn't do anymore.

So Julie grew up doing for others, just as she saw her mother caring for her family. If one of Julie's siblings needed advice or help, Julie was there to talk to them and care for them. Although she was the second youngest, she acted as if she were the mother. You see, Julie learned to get love by giving to others, and doing for others, not by doing for herself. Since her family was so large, most of her time was occupied in helping them.

When Julie was old enough to marry, she met a handsome, charming, rich man; and she fell madly in love with him. He was more than she ever imagined a man could be, and for the first time in her life she felt truly loved. But when he proposed to her, Julie couldn't say yes. She tried, but the words wouldn't come out. She thought, "Why would he want to marry me? He couldn't possibly love me like I love him. If I marry him, he will only hurt me. He must have another motive. I can't trust him."

As a child, Julie had not experienced being loved and cared for, so as an adult, she just couldn't believe that anyone could really love her. She was heartbroken when she turned him down, but at least she felt safe. Finally another handsome man proposed to her, and she said yes because he was safe. Julie didn't love him, but she knew if she married him, he wouldn't hurt her. Nothing could hurt her more than what she'd been through.

Julie caused her worst fear to happen. Sometimes people are so afraid of what will happen to them, they actually cause it to happen. They are too scared to move forward, too frightened to take risks.

Julie's story continued when her youngest daughter, Susan, also fell madly in love with a rich, handsome, and charming suitor. As Julie watched the relationship develop, her fear for her daughter surfaced as well. She watched Susan's relationship very closely. She told Susan, "He's going to hurt you, just like my boyfriend hurt me. He is too handsome to be trusted."

Susan believed her mother. She never stopped long enough to ask, "What does handsome have to do with trust? Why are you assuming that my relationship is like yours? Just because you were afraid to love, why should I be afraid?"

But Susan didn't ask these questions, instead she absorbed her mother's fears. The cycle repeated itself, although Julie was not aware she was passing her attitude toward life on to her daughter. In her mind she was just trying to protect her from being hurt. Susan turned away her suitor just as her mother had done thirty years before; and she also found a handsome man, like her father, to marry. He loved Susan more than she loved him. Therefore, she was safe, and wouldn't be hurt. History repeated itself, and Susan, like her mother, lived many years without feeling true love.

• • •

IMPACT in Action: Susan

I—I

"I don't deserve to be loved."

M—My

"My feelings are second to others."

P—Perception

Realizing how wrong she was, and how she had absorbed her mother's fears and attitude, Susan changed her perception by promising herself to break the cycle. Susan hoped her children would learn how to reach for what they wanted, and to get it.

A—Assumption

Susan faced her own inability to love her husband, and the difficulty of breaking a pattern her mother had so firmly established. She didn't give up; she began to question her own assumptions instead. This time it would be different. She would break the cycle, and find a way to allow herself to truly love the man she married. After all those years, he had proved that he deserved her love.

Attitude

In the process of learning how to let her husband's love in, Susan had to change her attitude. It was no longer good enough for her to believe as her mother did. She began to learn how to love herself, and to adopt the belief that she deserved love. Susan understood that if she didn't feel deserving of love, it would never come to her. It was up to her to ask for and get what she wanted. She was no longer going to live in fear.

Susan realized that her feelings of not deserving love and of doing for others were the fabric of her life. It had been woven for generations with many different colored threads. This three-generational fabric needed to be brought up-to-date and redesigned. Susan did not plan to change the part of herself that gave to others. She just wanted to add some new threads to the fabric which gave her permission to give to herself as well.

C—Communication

Susan decided to communicate her feelings to her husband. Since the fabric of living began with her parents, it was up to her to change it. She knew her parents did the best they could, and coming from their circumstances, it was more than enough. But Susan and her family represented a new generation, with new ideas; and even though her parents were good people, it was time for her to change the pattern.

T—Trust

Susan had to trust herself enough to persevere and to catch herself accepting love and help from others, not just giving it. It doesn't sound like a serious problem, but it had prevented Susan from filling the emptiness inside of her that had been with her a lifetime. She made a decision and made it work—easier said than done—but she did it.

Susan changed the dark side to the bright side, broke the three-generational pattern, and also taught her children a more fulfilling way of living. They got the love they deserved because she consciously showed them how special they were. They learned not to settle for less.

● ● ●

Part Two

~

Laws That Ensure Trust Between You and Your Child

~

Principles X–XIX

~ Chapter 13 ~

Principle X.

Say What You Mean and Mean What You Say

Make Your Words and Your Actions Match

To be congruent is to do what you say you are going to do. *When you say one thing and mean or do another, you are giving yourself and your children mixed messages that are confusing.* No wonder your children do not believe you, or listen to you! Think about it. Chances are that's what your parents did to you. Mixed messages are hereditary. They interfere with your ability to understand yourself, and your children's ability to understand and trust you. Mixed messages make you and them feel unsafe in the world. Be certain that what you say is exactly what you mean. Congruency means that your words and actions match.

Jim's mom said, "We're supposed to leave on vacation tomorrow—and all of a sudden, you're afraid of flying!" Then she took a deep breath, and said, "Thousands of planes take off and land safely every second. Planes are safer than cars." Jim began to feel better—until she finished with, "So what if our plane crashes, we won't know the difference anyway!" Wouldn't it have been better if she had left out that last sentence? It confused Jim by conveying exactly the opposite of what she intended. Be congruent—say what you mean, and mean what you say.

Your parents may have inadvertently given you mixed messages. They may have said one thing and done another. It's difficult not to make mistakes; we're human. But life can be a lot easier when we are willing to accept responsibility for our mistakes and demonstrate how we will fix them. Make your word your bond, and your children will learn to do the same.

Discuss the problem with your children. Learn why the mistake happened, and what each of you can do to correct your part in it. Decisions can be amended until they feel fair and work for each of you. As you set an example, give your children the benefit of the doubt. They will learn to do what you do. Remember, they've only been in your family a short time, so it will take a while for them to learn how to be what you want. They'll look to you and copy your behavior, as you copied your parents' behavior.

Take some time to think about it. What do you do that you know your parents did? Ask your partner, or friend. They'll be more honest with you than you can be with yourself. You are your children's most important model. The rewards for being congruent come back to you tenfold.

Congruency in Discipline

A perfect place to begin being congruent is in the way you discipline. You can discipline by setting boundaries. That means telling your children in advance, the consequences of what will happen when they don't listen. Giving them advance notice is a fair way of helping them to understand why it's important to listen, why it upsets you when they don't, and what you can do other than yell or scream. You can also ask them to suggest consequences they think will help them listen better. It's a fair issue to discuss and resolve together. Congruency in discipline is a building block in your relationship with them, and yourself. Your children gain control of their behavior by understanding yours.

When they are little, the consequences are small. As they grow older, the consequences increase as well. Each situation gives them experience to handle the next one better. A seven-year-old might be allowed to cross a small street in the neighborhood alone, but it wouldn't be appropriate for a four-year-old to do so. When you set boundaries, and discuss consequences, you and your children develop more ability and experience to handle new situations as they arise. Boundaries give your children some control over their behavior, and help them develop a desire to do better, because it feels good. They begin to understand what buttons they push when they go beyond boundaries, and why. Wouldn't you have felt a lot better if you had understood what made your mom or dad angry? Wouldn't you have been more secure around them when you realized they understood and didn't want to yell and scream at you?

How did going to your room help you correct your behavior? Wouldn't your children be proud of being able to talk through a discussion with you? If you explained why you were upset, and they explained why they were upset, wouldn't you both have gained respect for each other's feelings?

Changing boundaries through discussion and negotiation helps your children become more responsible and encourages a healthy relationship to develop. As they gain control over their actions, and knowledge of the consequences, their confidence in their ability to effect change grows. Wouldn't you both move closer to each other knowing you can work problems out? Would you have more fun and be more carefree as a result?

Temper Tantrums

You might have had temper tantrums as a child because you didn't understand something that happened, or perhaps what would happen next, or maybe the explanation you were given didn't make sense. I saw a Frisbee flying through the air the other day, and followed it. Just as it landed in the ocean, I heard little Mary shout, "Get the Frisbee, get the Frisbee." The water was frigid, and no one wanted to go in after it. But Mary kept crying, "I want my Frisbee. I want my Frisbee." Her mother promised to get her a new one because this one "is buried under the sand." It was clear the answer didn't make sense to her; it didn't make sense to me either. I knew the Frisbee was in the water only a few feet away. So did Mary.

Mary's parents walked on, hoping she would forget about the Frisbee. Mary's crying grew louder and more insistent. Her parents kept telling her that they'd buy her another one. No one understood. They walked on, ignoring her temper tantrum. If they had tried to retrieve the toy, she would have understood. But it was only a few feet away, and they didn't do anything. Mary was frustrated. Her parents' words and actions didn't match.

In her frustration, the mother blamed her older daughter for throwing the Frisbee into the water. The father came to her rescue, "It wasn't her fault. You always blame her." The family was divided.

Inconsistent parenting fuels temper tantrums, especially when the child does not understand the relationship between the incident and the consequences. When the world makes sense to children, there is little need to act out. All Mary's parents had to do was allow her to put her hands in the water. She wouldn't have wanted to go in after the Frisbee either. But they never gave her the chance to experience the consequences of retrieving the Frisbee.

A few days later I walked by the same beach, and noticed a flash of red jutting up from the rocks. Walking closer, I saw that it was the Frisbee. As I looked at it, I couldn't help think about how happy Mary would be to see her toy. What if her parents had told her they would come back another day to look for the Frisbee, after she had experienced them following through many times before? Even if they didn't find it, wouldn't she have felt better? Didn't she just want her feelings to matter? In Mary's eyes, if they cared about her Frisbee, then they cared about her. What message did they give her by dismissing the matter, and offering to buy another Frisbee? How much did the Frisbee affect Mary's trust in her parents? What did she learn about them?

Perhaps that they didn't always tell the truth or perhaps that they really didn't care about her feelings. Or maybe, "Parents don't always tell the truth, why should I?"

Most of us make early decisions about our lives in our first six years that affect the way we view our world. Right or wrong, it is our way of understanding the world. The problem is that we often continue to behave as toddlers, even when we're adults.

When the tables are turned, and you are very old, how do you want your children to treat you? Most likely they will give back just what you gave them.

Remember that your children will believe what you say to them. So be careful! They have their own thoughts. You don't own their thoughts and feelings, but you do own what you say to them, and how it affects what they believe about themselves. When you make disparaging remarks, there is a strong possibility your children will believe them. These remarks will then affect their attitude and their perception of themselves.

> *The greatest pleasure in life is doing what people say you cannot do.*
>
> WALTER BAGEHOT
> ENGLISH ECONOMIST AND JOURNALIST (1826–1877)

IMPACT Story: Marge

Marge's mother never saw her side of the situation. If Marge didn't do exactly as her mother said, she took it personally. "This child just wants to make my life miserable. I'll teach her that she can't talk to me this way." One day Marge overheard her mother tell her father that she was an impossible child who just had to do things her way. "She won't have any friends. Who would want to be with her?"

Marge did want to do things her way. But Marge wasn't being belligerent; she was being a five-year-old, and she was responding as a child. The adult in the situation had already initiated a power struggle. Mother couldn't understand that Marge was engaging in age-appropriate behavior. She was just testing her limits, and taking her first steps toward independence. Marge felt Mom just wouldn't listen to her. She always had to do what Mom wanted her to do. Secretly, Marge hated her mother.

When Marge was six she packed a bag and left home. Her father found her a few hours later, but Marge never forgot. She knew she was too little to leave home, but she began to question the kind of person she was. She thought, "Why doesn't Mom like me? What's wrong with me?" Marge didn't want to fight with her mother. She just wanted her mother to love her.

But her mother constantly told her, "You don't know everything. I'm smarter than you." And Marge believed her. When her mother asked her questions, and then tripped her up so that she answered them wrong, Marge felt stupid. Marge just wanted her mother to be a mom, like her friends' moms were.

Marge didn't know that her mother was competing with her for control. The child inside of her mother couldn't relate to Marge and felt threatened by Marge's rebellious nature. When Marge questioned authority by having an answer for everything, her mother didn't feel powerful enough to set boundaries and explain to Marge what she could or could not do, and why. The only way Mom knew how to feel grown up was by making Marge feel stupid. And finally Marge began to believe her mother.

When Marge was older, she realized that a power struggle was going on with her mother. But it didn't help the way she felt about herself. "When your mother says, 'I liked you until you began to talk,' you don't know. If you're not that little person looking up at this mother, you couldn't ever understand. Mother kept criticizing me. She kept saying, 'You're not as good as you think you are.' Now, as an adult, I interpret any questioning remark as criticism. I still don't feel as if I'm good enough."

When parents start to think differently, their children begin to see them differently. Why not tell our children what's good about them rather than what's wrong with them? Won't that affect how they perceive themselves, and us? Can our children be wrong all of the time? Can we be right all of the time?

• • •

IMPACT in Action: Marge

I—I
"I'm not good enough."

M—My
"There must be something wrong with me if my mother doesn't accept me."

P—Perception
Marge believed that people are not nice, and that they would always find something wrong with her. "I might as well just accept it. I'm better off being by myself. Life sucks. I'll stick with art."

A—Assumption
No matter how hard Marge tried, she assumed there was something wrong with her. She longed for a relationship with her mother but it grew worse as she grew older. The more her mother criticized her, the less time she spent with her. Even birthdays were difficult. Her mother would give her a gift, and then spend the rest of their time together telling her what was wrong with her, and how much nicer other people's children were.

Attitude
As Marge's mother grew older, she desperately wanted a relationship with her daughter. Each time they were together Marge had an attitude. She expected her mother to criticize her, and wasn't disappointed. When Mom criticized Marge walked away; she had to protect herself. Marge was an adult. She wasn't going to allow herself to be abused by her mother anymore.

But Marge had an attitude toward others as well. She found herself on the defensive most of the time in order to avoid the painful critical attacks she had suffered as a child. She had an emptiness inside of her that was difficult to fill. The emptiness came from having a mother who never showed her love and appreciation.

Marge had a difficult time with others because of her rebellious attitude. She wore the wounds her mother left her as a badge of honor. Marge's rebelliousness prevented her from having a fulfilling career as well. She did, however, develop very close and loving friendships because she chose her few friends with extreme caution.

C—Communication

Marge worked hard on communicating with her children because she wanted them to understand their world. She knew how important communication was, because of her own desperate need for understanding when she was a child. She vowed to give her children what she had missed as a child. She knew how important it was to tell her children good things about themselves, because she understood how devastating criticism was. She used words very carefully. Marge took the time to say what she meant.

T—Trust

By the time Marge was a mother, she had reversed her childhood patterns. She had learned what *not to do* to her children from her mother. When she raised her own children, she intuitively understood how they felt. She allowed them to have their feelings; she knew how important they were to them. She gave her children the trust she wished her mother had given her.

• • •

~ Chapter 14 ~

Principle XI.
Follow Through

Following through is the most obvious principle to grasp, and the hardest one to follow. (You might have heard this concept a zillion times, but still do not do it.) It's difficult to do what you said you would do. Did your parents? You might remember many times when they said one thing and did another. You may have gotten used to it. Or you might have hardly noticed when it was happening. But it did affect the way you listened to them, and how you were disciplined. Your parents may still make statements that contradict each other so you've decided on your own way of doing things. The problem is that you do to your children what your parents did to you because you are not consciously aware of all that happened when you were little; yet it is stored within you, like a computer, and comes out when the right button is pressed.

What Happens If You Don't?: Peter and Juan

Your children quickly discover whether you follow through, and behave accordingly. Ask yourself if you are like Peter's parents, or Juan's.

Peter's mom said he couldn't have candy until after dinner. But when they were shopping, and he was tired, she would give him candy. It was easier to give in to Peter than to listen to the same questions over and over. To Peter that meant, "If I keep asking, I'll get what I want."

When his mother said he had to go to bed on time, Peter thought, "She won't stick with it. Sometimes she doesn't mind when I stay up late." In Peter's mind he had permission to keep checking on her. When she gave in, he won; when she didn't, he cried. Her inconsistency created a power struggle with no winners and lots of unhappiness.

Juan's mom, on the other hand, stuck to bedtime, dinner time, treat time, and so on. Juan knew that if his mother let him stay up late, it was for a good reason; and he was grateful for the opportunity. It didn't pay to test her because she always kept her word, and when she didn't, she explained why she was making an exception. Because he knew what would happen next, he didn't need to throw temper tantrums. All he had to do was ask when he didn't understand. Her answers made him feel secure, and he behaved in the same way.

Peter would cry and scream until he got what he wanted by wearing his mother down. His parents finally realized that giving in wasn't easier. In the end, it was even more difficult; Peter became more spoiled day by day. Although they loved him, they began to like him less. When they wondered if Peter would act this way as a teenager and an adult, the thought sobered them. They realized that if they didn't help Peter change his behavior, it would grow with him, and he could become a very difficult adult to deal with. The thought gave them the courage to stay with their resolve, and the patience to teach Peter another way to get what he wanted.

When the tantrums came again as expected, his father gave it a try instead of his mother. He was prepared, and said, "Peter, you don't have to scream. Just ask. Screaming stops you from getting what you want." Of course Peter continued to scream. Then Dad said, "Let's put it in writing, and see what happens. If you ask I will help you get what you want. When you scream, you have no chance. Would you like to start again, and ask for what you want?" When Peter screamed again, Dad said, "Didn't we write down that you could get ice cream after dinner if you didn't scream? Now it's before dinner, you wanted ice cream and I said no, and you cried. Let's read what we wrote: 'You could have ice cream when you asked, if it was after dinner and if you didn't scream.' So no ice cream today. We'll try again tomorrow. But if you scream again, you won't get ice cream."

The next day, before Peter could demand what he wanted, his father reminded him of their agreement and the consequences. Peter thought for a minute, and then asked politely for ice cream. His father followed through, as promised. After repeated lessons, he learned to ask politely, and began to get what he wanted. In the beginning Dad gave Peter small rewards that reinforced his good behavior. After a while Peter realized he had no need to scream, and in fact, screaming made things worse.

His father's secret weapon was that he kept his word, and wrote down what he said, so he could show it to Peter. He said what he meant and meant what he said, and *followed through with what he said he would do*. When Peter realized that Dad was consistent, he gradually stopped screaming and demanding. Both parents knew he had developed this bad habit because they had found it easier to give in than to put up with the tantrums, and they weren't consistent. Now they had to undo their mistakes, and help Peter develop better habits before it was too late. Even so, Dad was surprised when Peter's tantrums diminished. He finally realized that children need to feel understood. They need to be given what they are promised, then they can be accepting, and forgiving.

What if Dad hadn't found a way to help Peter get what he wanted, as he had promised? Would Peter believe him and listen to him in the future? Or would Peter continue his temper tantrums? At least they worked temporarily! What do you think?

Parents are not perfect. Sometimes parents make promises they don't remember. Don't be misled into thinking your children won't remember the promises you make. When it happens, take responsibility. When your children realize it's an honest mistake, and you're willing to correct it, you'll be amazed at how under-standing they can be.

It's not unusual for children to change the facts so that cir-cumstances work to their advantage. In truth, they honestly believe they are right. Rules elude them unless you make a spe-cific effort to point them out.

Let's listen to Ryan and his mother.

> **Ryan:** *Mom, you said I could have a friend over today if I cleaned my room.*
> **Mom:** *I didn't say today.*
> **Ryan:** *Yes, you did, Mom, and now you're telling me no. That's not fair. What about my friend?"*

Although Ryan's mom felt she was right, she gave her son the benefit of the doubt.

> **Mom:** *If you think I said today then there must be a misunderstanding. I'll have to be clearer the next time. Today will be difficult for me, but a promise is a promise, we'll work it out. If you'd like I'll let you have two friends tomorrow to make up for this mistake, or one friend today. Which do you choose?*
> **Ryan:** *What'll I do if I don't have my friend over today?*
> **Mom:** *We'll talk about it and come up with some-thing interesting.*
> **Ryan:** *Okay, I'll choose tomorrow.*
> **Mom:** *Next time, I think I'll write my promise down so there's no misunderstanding. Is that okay with you?*
> **Ryan:** *Sure, Mom, that's a great idea.*
> **Mom:** *Will you write your promises down too?*

Notice how Ryan's mom has just given the responsibility to Ryan as well as to herself. Whose responsibility is it anyway, yours or your children's, or both? She also subtly introduced her son to contracts (Principle XXIII). Wasn't that better than telling him she didn't believe him? Now each of them can take 50 percent of the responsibility for their misunderstandings, and the contracts will help them build a trusting relationship with each other, providing Ryan's mom follows through. If she doesn't, she'll know why her son doesn't listen. Would you blame him? After all, a promise is a promise is a promise.

Learn the art of patience. Apply discipline to your thoughts when they become anxious over the outcome of a goal. Impatience breeds anxiety, fear, discouragement and failure.

Patience creates confidence, decisiveness and a rational outlook, which eventually leads to success.
                                                          BRIAN ADAMS

IMPACT Story: Doug

Doug was always in trouble, either with his mother or father. He didn't know what was wrong with him. He was only five. Why was life so difficult?

One day when Doug was playing with me, he asked, "How come I'm always good when I'm with you, and when I'm at my grandmom's?" I answered, "You're very good when you're with me. You take turns. When you want to do things your way, and I want a turn to do what I want, we talk about it. We decide to play half your way and half my way. We always have fun, don't we?" Doug told me he liked playing with me. I said, "You're a good boy. And when it's time to go home, you always put your toys away. I like when you do that." Doug's face lit up—he was so proud.

Then Doug said, "My mommy tells me to put my pajamas on, and if I don't do it when she tells me, she says that she's going to make me sleep in the woods with the bears." He looked scared. I reassured him that his mother wouldn't make him sleep in the woods. He said, "I know," but the fear was still there.

When Doug's mom came to take him home I heard her tell him to clean up, and put his jacket on. When he didn't respond as quickly as she wanted, she said, "Okay, I'm leaving. You can go home with Eydie."

I decided to take Doug's mother aside and explain to her that Doug was a literal thinker. "He believes that you might leave him, and that scares him. You're his mother and he's been waiting for you to come get him and take him home." She laughed. "You should have heard the horrid statements my mother said to me."

I knew her well enough to be able to point out that she had just done the same thing to Doug. She was astonished. I asked, "Didn't you once tell me you were a bad kid, always getting into trouble because of your attitude?" She laughed and agreed. Then I asked her, "How did Doug respond when you told him to go home with me?" She said, "He stuck out his tongue and made a face."

I told her about our earlier conversation. She just didn't realize she was scaring him just as her parents had scared her. "Thanks. I'll work on not doing that anymore. But I'm so used to it, I don't even realize what I'm saying."

• • •

IMPACT in Action: Doug

I—I
"I'm bad."

M—My
"My mommy and daddy think I'm bad. I must be bad if they say so."

P—Perception
Doug perceives that he can't do anything right because he's always getting into trouble.

A—Assumption
He assumes that he might as well do as he wants. "I'll get into trouble no matter what I do."

Attitude
Doug's always angry because he assumes no one likes him.

C—Communication
Doug started communicating his feelings, and his parents listened. It took some time until Doug recognized that he wasn't such a bad boy after all, and he slowly changed.

T—Trust
Doug's parents began changing the way they responded to their son. They learned that saying things they didn't mean hurt him; he was sensitive and a literal thinker. Doug took their words seriously even when they didn't. He was so intelligent that when his parents made outrageous statements, he pictured them doing exactly what they said. "If they would make me sleep with the bears, then they don't love me." No wonder he was scared and angry most of the time. Thinking he was bad just made things worse.

His parents helped each other change as well. The more they told Doug that he was good, the better he behaved. His father found it hard to believe that his son had an ego. I said, "He certainly does. He's very bright, and needs to be spoken to with respect. You can see that he behaves better when he realizes how important he is to you."

• • •

The hardest part of raising children for any of us is to constantly follow through. When Doug's parents followed through, over and over again, he began to trust them. Their relationship with him, and with their younger son, and with each other, changed dramatically. Once they were able to follow through by meaning what they said, and saying what they meant, their actions and family grew in the positive direction they had always imagined.

Chapter 15

Principle XII.
The Key to Happiness Is Balance

Balance means to be good enough to your children, but not too good or not good enough—when you are too good, your children can become spoiled or selfish, and unwittingly take advantage of your generosity; when you aren't good enough, your children may lack self-esteem. Being good enough means giving enough to your children so they are nurtured and loved, but not so much that they don't have the confidence to earn things for themselves.

When you wanted something special, did your parents say no or just ignore you, or did they give you the opportunity to earn it? Did they give you jobs that helped you earn enough money to reach your goals, or did they make it so hard that you gave up? When you help your children gain the confidence to achieve small goals, they'll be able to tackle larger ones naturally. Remember: Help them, but don't do it for them. Of course goals need to be age-appropriate. Five-year-olds do not care about money; they want immediate satisfaction. So make a deal for help around the house. You can say, "Joel, as soon as you can put your toys neatly on the shelf, we'll go to the park." Or if you're teaching the concept of earning, you can say, "When you put your toys away all by yourself without me asking, Joel, I'll buy you the sticker you wanted." At age seven, you might want to teach them how to save enough money to buy a reward themselves. It's important to teach your children that they can earn what they want, even at an early age. Your child, at age five, will be proud that he earned a new sticker, while seven-year-old Cindy might want to earn enough to buy a new coloring book. A reward for a seven-year-old can be stretched over a week—but not much more. It's not important that rewards be expensive. Actually, the less they cost, the better. It's the concept that matters, not the cost. When you meet your children halfway, you help them develop purpose in their lives, and confidence in themselves, by knowing they worked and achieved their goals at each stage of their life.

For centuries, the maxim was, Spare the rod, and spoil the child. Physical punishment and stern, strict treatment were not unusual. Children were to be seen and not heard. Sigmund Freud, the father of psychology, helped reverse much of that philosophy. Many parents took too much responsibility. They feared that whatever they did would ruin their children. From the mid-1950s to the mid-1970s, parents spoiled their children. Overindulgence coupled with the easier times following World War II produced the "me" generation and the greed of the 1980s. Now it's time to create a balance between giving enough, but not too much, teaching our children responsibility, associating consequences with their own actions, and developing a realistic way to learn rather than to punish—certainly a worthwhile endeavor for the next millennium.

Learning to Give

We should learn to give without expecting anything in return; the giver becomes the receiver by experiencing the satisfaction of giving. We can encourage our children to do the same by keeping balance in mind. Giving and goodness comes back in abundance. The universe sees to it that what we give out is exactly what we get back, in one way or another. However, we must teach our children that we do not get it back at that very moment, but through

becoming good people. As goodness attracts and breeds goodness, good people will naturally flow into our lives. Also, giving
teaches giving. When we give continually without finding balance
or pausing to teach our children how to give, we spoil them. For
example, complimenting them and appreciating their actions is
very important. These rewards are far more important than giving
material things. But if you compliment indiscriminately, they may
take the praise for granted and come to expect it rather than to
earn it. It is important to strive for balance in everything we do,
from raising our children to caring for ourselves.

Showing gratitude and appreciation to our children teaches
them as well. For example, Sammi made a large multicolored picture of a barnyard as a Grandparent's Day gift. Her grandpa
adored it. "Oh, Sammi, thank you, it's beautiful." Guess what he
didn't say—"Whoever heard of a purple cow?" He may have
thought it, but he didn't say it, because he knew how important
it was to show appreciation, and to not be critical of what she did.
It meant a lot to Sammi. When Grandpa said, "I really appreciate
it when you think of me," Sammi fairly burst with pride. She
hadn't really thought of drawing the picture; her mom had suggested it. Sammi learned several lessons that day.

When Dad was taking over for Mom one day, he said to
Raul, "Thank you so much for helping with the dishes, it gives
me more time to be with you," Raul was as proud as Sammi. And
it helped his self-confidence to be so important to his father.
When Raul was careless, his father found the one dish that he had
taken his time with, and said, "I like the way you made this dish
sparkle." The rest of the dishes looked a lot better after that.

Our behavior teaches our children what to do. When they
receive compliments from us, they are able to give compliments
to others. They learn from what we do, not what we say to do.
When we are good to our children, they are good to others. We
are their models.

I never told my children, "Say thank you", but I always said
"please" and "thank you" to them. When their teachers told me
how polite they were, I knew it was from following my example.

I feel embarrassed for children when their parents say, "Now, say thank you." They'll get it. Just give them a chance.

It isn't necessary to tell our children to be grateful for what we do or give them. It only embarrasses them and makes them feel guilty for what we have done for them. For example, Mom bought Matt a model car, and a new shirt, and a kickball for his birthday. Let's eavesdrop on their conversation.

> **Matt:** *But, Mom, I wanted a football. Why didn't you buy me the football I asked for?*

His mother saw that Matt's remark showed that he didn't appreciate the other things she gave him, but she didn't call him selfish and spoiled.

> **Mom:** *When you appreciate what I give you, and I see how happy you are, I want to give you more. But when you ask for more, I get angry, and I feel like giving you less.*
>
> **Matt:** *Mom, I really love the car you gave me, and the shirt. I'm sorry that I didn't say thank you for the kickball. I was just disappointed because I wanted the football so much.*
>
> **Mom:** *Thank you, Matt. I know you appreciate what I do for you. I didn't realize how disappointed you would be by not getting the football for your birthday. I was planning to buy it for Christmas.*
>
> **Matt:** *It's okay, Mom. I saved some money, and I would really like to buy it now because the kids won't be able to play football when it snows. May I?*

Mom understood. Next time she'll be a little more perceptive about why he wants things. She realized Matt was the kind child she raised him to be. She was glad she hadn't called him selfish and greedy, and had taken the time to explain things to him and to understand where he was coming from. Our actions will speak louder than our words.

*Your automatic creative mechanism is teleological.
That is, it operates in terms of goals and end
results. Once you give it a definite goal to achieve
you can depend upon its automatic guidance
system to take you to that goal much better than
you ever could by conscious thought.*

*You supply the goal by thinking in terms of end
results. Your automatic mechanism then supplies
the means whereby.*

MAXWELL MALTZ
PHYSICIAN, SELF-IMAGE PSYCHOLOGY

Find the Balance in Your Life

Have you ever stopped to think that your children learn how to be adults by watching the way you are as an adult and the way you live your life? When your children are little, they are more intuitive and sensitive than you can imagine. They have their little antennas out all of the time so they can learn about their world. They live their life through their feelings. They know what feels right, and what feels wrong—and they remember those feelings. Some children grow up to be conscious of their childhood, and knowing how they want to live their adulthood. Other children do not want to remember their childhood; but the pain of it is buried in their minds, and it surfaces in the way they treat other people and the way they treat themselves.

Have you envisioned the kind of person you hope your child will become? Although your child has come into this world equipped with his own strengths and weaknesses, he or she will absorb your values. Your child learns how to read and write in school, but how to be a person at home.

Do you value the other people in your life? Are you able to show them how much they mean to you by giving attention to their needs? Or do you want people to listen to you, and what you have to say, but you don't have the time to listen to them, or see their needs as important? Do you show your love by buying your children clothes and toys rather than by spending time with them and showing them how much you value who they are?

If you see people as important, and value them, your child will learn to do the same. Or do you value possessions more than people? If so, when your child becomes an adult he will learn that buying new toys for himself is more important than how he treats you and the other people in his life.

Have you found a way to balance the time you spend giving special attention and love to your family, career, personal relaxation, physical activities, and your health? If you have created balance in your life, you are ensuring that your children will do the same. They learn how to live their life by watching you. How did you learn? If you work most of the time, and rarely have time to be with your children, do you think they'll find the time to spend with you when you are older and appreciate being with them more? They are going to do just what you do. If you are excessive in your work and play, they may be the same way as adults because that's what they have seen.

Some adults feel so bad about the way their parents treated them that they make a conscious effort to be the parent they always wanted rather than the parent they had. They can achieve the life they always wanted as a child when they constantly remember the way their parents were, and use it as a model of how not to be.

The way you will live your life will guide your children to the way they will live their lives. The way you treat your children will come back to you. They will give you exactly what you asked for. Be careful what you ask for, you just might get it.

IMPACT Story: Uncle Morris

Although Uncle Morris was my husband's uncle, I think of him as mine because the messages he gave me changed my life. As a very special client was leaving my office one day, he pointed to a picture of Uncle Morris and asked, "Who is he?" I thought it was an interesting question since we had spent the past hour discussing spirituality, and the opportunities that arise when we choose to believe in a higher purpose that exists outside of ourselves.

I told my client about Uncle Morris, and how he not only had a dramatic effect on my life but helped many other lives as well. Uncle Morris died in November 1963, shortly after President Kennedy's death. Fourteen years earlier the doctors had given him six months to live. As a young man, although he wanted to be a doctor, Uncle Morris dropped out of college to help support his younger brother and sisters. He became a very successful businessman and helped many people he came in contact with. He encouraged them to express their feelings and he helped them in other ways, often financially as well. Uncle Morris provided an example of living with understanding and peace. Although he wasn't a celebrity, several miles of cars joined his funeral procession, and hundreds of people stood in the rain outside the crowded funeral parlor to pay their respects. I had admired Uncle Morris for who he was, and the many ways he helped my husband and me.

I was twenty-one and newly married, and I had hoped people would love and accept me as my parents had. I didn't know people could be any other way, but it didn't take long to realize that it wasn't going to happen. My parents were loving and accepting, but I was running into nasty, critical people who thought that whatever we did wasn't good enough. *And at that age, I took it personally.* I thought that if I was a better person and could please others, they would accept and love me.

I was so frustrated that I called Aunt Jenny, Uncle Morris's wife, and asked her how to handle a family situation. Within a few hours, Uncle Morris was on the telephone asking us to his house for dinner. Shortly after, we were in the car with him and Aunt Jenny accompanying them on a trip. To this day, I can vividly remember Uncle Morris asking me why I was upset. I couldn't believe that he cared enough to ask. I had only spoken to Aunt Jenny for a few minutes that afternoon. He listened patiently and then explained, "Eydie, don't take it personally. There are people who do the same thing to me. I give them my time, money, clothes, and furniture, but whatever I do, they find a reason to complain. That's who they are. But I don't do it for them. I do it for myself. Because I know I'm a good person, and I feel good about that. I do what's right. Then nobody can tell me anything different."

• • •

IMPACT in Action: Edythe

I—I

"Whatever I do isn't good enough."

M—My

"I need to be accepted, appreciated, and loved."

P—Perception

My perception was that if people didn't appreciate me, it must have been because I did something wrong.

A—Assumption

I assumed that if other people weren't nice to me it was because there was something wrong with me. I just wasn't good enough. But I didn't know why.

Attitude

My feelings about what other people said to me hurt me and made me angry. These feelings blocked my ability to express myself. When Uncle Morris communicated his feelings to me, my perception and then my attitude changed. I spent the next thirty years working on not taking other people's criticisms personally.

I learned that when I stepped out of my circumstances, I was able to see other people using the same critical, nasty behavior on their own family as they had used on me. Uncle Morris was right. It wasn't personal. It was just the way some people are.

T—Trust

On that day, Uncle Morris taught me to trust my own instincts. I would no longer allow others to determine who I was. My work from that day forward enabled me to strive toward bringing balance into my life.

My mother had always overlooked the way others treated her. She had treated others well because she felt it was the right way to be. I hadn't wanted to listen to her because I grew up thinking that people had taken advantage of her good nature. But Uncle Morris put it in perspective: "I do what's right because I don't do it for them, I do it for myself. That way I can feel good about who I am, and I don't have to take their criticism personally."

• • •

I have learned that some people are willing to look at themselves, and grow and change so they can be accountable for what they say and do. Others are not yet ready or able to have that kind of insight. They are so absorbed in themselves and their lives that they can't see beyond where they are. That's okay. They can be them, and I will be me. By constantly trying to be aware of the higher self in myself and others, I am able to obtain the balance and peace I desire. Try it. You may enjoy the feelings you receive. You may like it.

∼ Chapter 16 ∼

Principle XIII.

Talk about It Because It Won't Go Away

After having dinner at a friend's house, Walter commented to his wife, "Their family is so close." Ruth replied, "Funny, I was thinking along those lines too. When I noticed how easily they spoke with each other, I thought of how uncommunicative our children are. We've been calling it the generation gap—and teenage rebellion." "Yes," said Walter, "Where is the generation gap there? Do you remember how we used to tease our friends for spending so much time explaining things to their children, and how we thought it was overdone?" Ruth replied, "I sure do. We didn't talk about anything with our children. We just punished them when they didn't listen. Now they're too old to punish, and look at what is happening. Do you think our friends knew something we didn't?"

Walter replied, "Maybe it's not too late to change things with our children. All our problems started when they wouldn't listen to us. Could it be that we never heard them when they were growing up. Is that what causes the generation gap?"

Learning about Death

Failure to communicate with your children can affect the way they view their world when they become adults. For example, what do we say about death? Sandra's grandfather had a conversation with her that she will value forever:

> *Sandra:* Grandpa, are you going to die?
>
> *Grandpa:* Someday, sure. Everybody dies.
>
> *Sandra:* Mom's dad died. He was a nice guy. Where'd he go?
>
> *Grandpa:* Some people say there's a place called heaven.
>
> *Sandra:* When you die are you going to go to heaven?
>
> *Grandpa:* I hope so, honey.
>
> *Sandra:* Well, if you go to heaven, will I go to heaven too?
>
> *Grandpa:* I'd say so.
>
> *Sandra:* How will you recognize me? I'll be much older then.
>
> *Grandpa:* Honey, I'll always recognize you.
>
> *Sandra:* Grandpa, how will I talk to you when you go to heaven?
>
> *Grandpa:* Just remember to look up at a star, and I'll be there watching you. I'll know when you look for me. And if you need help, just ask me. I'll help you.
>
> *Sandra:* How will you hear me?
>
> *Grandpa:* I'll hear everything that's important. Sometimes, it takes time, so keep asking. The answers will come. You just have to remember that I love you very much, and that I'll help you even though you can't hear me. Just remember me, and I'll be there for you. Death is a part of life, Sandra. Just as we know the sun will rise and set each day, we also know that we will be born and we will die. I love you, honey.
>
> *Sandra:* I love you too, Grandpa.

Do you remember wondering about death as a child? Most kids play games where everyone dies, and then they're alive again the next minute. If they're not given toy guns to play with, they'll use their fingers to shoot with. It's their way of exploring what it is all about. Were you allowed to ask about death or was it a subject that was not discussed?

If death was explained to you as a child and talked about, you probably came to accept it and didn't develop a terrible fear of it. But if you were not allowed to talk about someone you loved who died (i.e., a grandparent or a friend), you are probably having a difficult time with it today. For many of us, it becomes one of our deepest fears. If we are able to talk about death, and ask the questions we need to ask to those we love so much, wouldn't we be more able to accept its inevitability? Wouldn't that help us enjoy and appreciate life with each other more? When Sandra's grandfather dies, she'll remember the conversation she had with him. She will look up into the sky, fix her eyes on one of the stars, and whisper, "Grandpa, I know you can hear me, even when I can't hear you. I know you'll always be there for me."

How do you suppose Fred learned about his mother's death? He had spent the summer in camp, and when he came home he learned that his mother had died. He was devastated. "I knew that Mom had cancer and that she had been sick for a long time, but if she were close to dying, why did they send me away? She disappeared from my life without me ever knowing it." Fred's sense of security was badly damaged. After that he continually feared the unexpected, and couldn't relax or enjoy each day, and he had trouble trusting people. Would his life have been different if he had known of his mother's impending death and had been to her funeral? Would talking about it then have changed his need to face it over and over today? Fred walks around with an underlying fear, always expecting something to happen. The unknown is worse than the known. Not knowing causes us to fantasize answers that are worse than the truth. We begin to "catastrophize," to coin a word. Isn't it more frightening to think that people will just disappear rather than to know why they die?

Debbie's mother had a similar early experience, and her feelings taught her not to do the same with her children. Debbie said, "Mommy, can I see great-grandmother before she dies?" Mother didn't know what to say, and she was frightened. She didn't think Debbie knew her great-grandmother was dying. No one talked about it. Her husband said, "Definitely not." Debbie kept asking. Her mother remembered not being allowed to ask questions when she was a child. At twenty-four, she was too frightened to go to her grandmother's funeral. She threw up in the car on the way there, and felt ashamed all the way home, because she loved her grandma more than anyone else. Remembering her own feelings, Debbie's mom took her to see her great-grandmother, even though everybody opposed it. In her heart she knew she was doing the right thing.

Zack was in California when his fifteen-year-old dog was dying. His mother called him to let him know, asked if she should let the vet put his old friend to sleep, or wait until he came home. She knew that encouraging him to make his own decisions would help him face his own grief.

Zack's mom had had the same experience. Her old dog was put to sleep while she was at school one day. Nobody had asked her. And it was a long time before she could forgive her parents for that; she lost trust and respect as well. Zack was heartbroken the day his dog died. His mother asked him to think of both the good and the bad. He said, "My dog was old, and wasn't feeling well anymore. He needed to stop hurting. I'll miss him. That's the bad. The good was that I was lucky to have a dog that loved me so much. I learned how to love animals from him." Then his mother suggested that in a few months they look for another puppy. "But we won't look for it now. Now is the time to wait and see."

Life affords no higher pleasure than that of surmounting difficulties, passing from one step of success to another, forming new wishes and seeing them gratified.
                                        Samuel Johnson
                              English writer (1709–1784)

IMPACT Story: Roger

When Roger's mother died, no one talked about it. Roger could see his father was heartbroken, and he didn't want to cause him more pain, so he kept his feelings to himself. Dad didn't ask him about them either. Each night Roger cried himself to sleep, hoping there was a God, and that his mom heard him. But Roger really felt alone. His older brother was away at college and he didn't talk about his mom's death either when he came home. That's just the way it was, and Roger's sadness remained inside of him. He did a wonderful job of not showing his feelings.

Roger fed and dressed himself in the morning, did his chores, walked to school by himself, and did his homework at day's end. In fact, his only outlet was school. He was extremely bright, athletic, and personable. When Roger excelled in baseball, his father didn't attend any of his games. He was busy working. Although Roger's aunt was kind and communicative, she couldn't fill the empty place.

Roger survived, as we all do, and later married a very special woman, Rhonda. She was there for him in a way no one had been before. Her actions showed Roger that she loved him, but she didn't know how to use words to tell him. The loneliness of childhood remained within him. He felt his partner was there, but not there for him.

Rhonda had grown up in a home where she saw her brothers get into trouble when they expressed their feelings. Her mom and dad weren't interested in feelings. Since Rhonda was the middle child she learned quickly that it was best to keep her feelings to herself so she wouldn't get into trouble like her brothers.

Although Rhonda loved Roger more than anything in the world, she couldn't express it. She just didn't know how. It was hard to break the habit of silence. When Roger told Rhonda how much he needed her to talk to him, she understood, but didn't do anything about it. Each time Roger expressed himself, he was left with a feeling of rejection. It reminded him of the way his dad had treated him after his mother died. When Roger couldn't escape the loneliness anymore, he sought counseling. He felt foolish. He was in a good marriage, but he was still so unhappy.

Take the time to talk to your children, even when it hurts. It is far less painful in the long run than it can possibly be to bury the feelings today. Your feelings are there for a reason. Find the reason. You and your family deserve it. You are important, and your feelings are an important part of you.

• • •

IMPACT in Action: Roger

I—I
"I'm not important."

M—My
"My feelings don't count."

P—Perception
Roger perceives that other people are more important than him.

A—Assumption
He assumes that if he doesn't talk about his pain, it will go away.

Attitude
Roger realizes that the pain doesn't go away. "I feel sad and alone."

C—Communication
When Roger's wife started talking to him about her feelings, it helped Roger open up and express himself. Although nothing really changed, somehow Roger felt different. He wasn't as lonely as he was before.

T—Trust
Roger trusted himself enough to believe that his feelings did count, and they were important. Rhonda agreed. Each of them brought a new dimension to their children, and each found a happier way of being.

• • •

~ Chapter 17 ~

Principle XIV.

Don't Just "Hear" What Your Children Are Saying— "Listen" to Them

Although you've been told to listen to your children, you may not have experienced what it's like for someone to really hear you. When someone hears what you meant, and not what they think you meant, it feels very good. Most of us put our own meaning into what someone else is saying.

Mirroring

Although Anthony's father knew how important it was to really hear what his son was saying, he had a difficult time communicating with him. Anthony was often very fresh to his mother when his father wasn't around. When Dad was there, Anthony would purposely do the opposite of what he was told, and would take his time doing it as well. It seemed as if he just wanted to aggravate his father. But his mother knew that Anthony was upset because his father worked so much and was rarely home. When she tried to talk to her son about it, it just didn't work. She knew it had to come from his father.

Anthony's father had faith in his wife's intuition and agreed to talk with his son. But since he wasn't around very much, he didn't want to be angry with Anthony when he was there. His wife told him about a communication style called "mirroring," developed by Dr. Harville Hendrix, an expert on the subject. "Mirroring" is repeating the essence of another person's thoughts, making sure to change the wording so the technique isn't obvious. This method of listening helps the person feel as if they are being heard, believed, and respected.

Anthony's father knew that he wouldn't have much luck talking to his son any other way at this point. He really wanted to reach his son, so he gave it a try. At first he felt uneasy paraphrasing everything Anthony said to him. Then he noticed that Anthony began to feel safe enough to express his feelings. Let's see how it helped them communicate.

Not knowing quite how to begin, Dad asked Anthony why he took so long to get ready to go to the store with him. Anthony ignored him for a long time. His father persisted, and Anthony finally said, "I don't want to go with you. [That was obvious.] You don't really want to be with me. If you did you wouldn't always be working."

Setting aside his anger at the response, his father mirrored Anthony's feelings. The technique uses specific stem sentences and progresses something like this:

"If I hear you right, you think (or feel)…"

He makes sure that Anthony acknowledges him by asking, "Is that right?"

Pausing for an answer, he then asks, "Is there more about that?"

Paraphrasing again, he says, "So, if I hear you correctly, you think (or feel)…"

Next, he validates, "I can see that you're upset because…"

Finally, he empathizes, "I can imagine how I would feel if I thought my dad…"

This technique helped Anthony open up because he felt his father was really listening to him. Now let's eavesdrop on the conversation:

> **Dad:** *If I hear you right, you're really angry that I'm always working.*
>
> **Anthony** (relaxing because his dad hears him): *Yeah that's right.*
>
> **Dad:** *Is there more about that?*
>
> **Anthony:** *Why don't you want to play with me?*
>
> **Dad:** *So you think I don't want to play with you. Is that right?*
>
> **Anthony:** *Yeah, that's right. If you did, you'd be home more.*
>
> **Dad:** *Is there more about that?*
>
> **Anthony:** *No.*
>
> **Dad** (summarizing Anthony's view): *So if I hear you correctly, you think I don't want to play with you and that's why I work all the time.*
>
> **Anthony:** *Yeah, that's right.*
>
> **Dad** (validating Anthony's feelings before presenting his own): *I can see that you must feel very hurt when you think I don't want to be with you and that's why I'm always working.*
>
> **Anthony** *looks down at the ground and sighs.*
>
> **Dad** (empathizing): *I can imagine that it must feel pretty awful to think that your dad doesn't really love you.*

When Anthony nodded again, Dad knew that this was the time to explain why he worked so much, and he did. Anthony looked up at him, wiped away his tears, and gave him a big hug. He heard his father say how much he loved him and why he was working so much. He was glad his father had given him the chance to express his feelings. Anthony didn't know why he was so angry until the words came out. Now he felt better, "Let's go Dad, I'm ready."

After that Dad and Anthony planned special times together in between Dad's difficult work hours. They also wrote contracts that helped them repair their relationship by trusting each other to keep his word. (See Principle XXIII, p. 186) Most important, they talked, which helped both of them.

As you can see, hearing your children will calm them, and encourage them to express their feelings. Mirroring your child's feelings helps them feel safe, and they won't be criticized for what they say.

When your children can express their feelings to you without worrying about being judged, criticized, or told what to do, they will feel free to talk more, and to trust that you really care about what they have to say. It takes work on your part, and may seem unnatural at first. However, the results may change your mind. Most of us have a hard time communicating and find it even more difficult to teach our children how to express their feelings. (This method may also be very helpful in healing and strengthening your marriage. Ask your spouse or close friend to try mirroring with you so you have an idea of what being heard feels like.)

The questions your children ask may be their way of expressing a deeper worry. By listening to what they are asking, you may find clues to what they are feeling.

My son was born on December 7, Pearl Harbor Day. Often when he was asked his age and his birthday, people would respond, "Oh, Pearl Harbor Day!" or "You poor thing. Oh what a terrible day to be born on!" One night he asked me why people looked sad when he said December 7. "What is Pearl Harbor Day?"

I am grateful that I was able to hear what was beneath his words. My answer helped him toward the path he would pursue during his lifetime. It helped him to feel good about who he was, and to find a solid reason for being born on December 7. I said, "War happened on that day. You were born on that day so you could bring good things to the world. The world needs people like you to make things better." He asked a lot of questions about war after that. He also began to do little things to help his friends. As an adult he became a psychologist to continue helping people.

Because of his belief that he was put here for a reason, he is spiritual, kind, and loving. People tell me they can feel the goodness in him when they meet. What if no one had heard and understood the impact his birthday had on him? Could it have caused him to feel bad about what his birthday stood for, and who he was?

When you really hear what your children are saying, good things will happen. You are encouraging your children to feel important. Their behavior will rise to your expectations, and will bring enjoyment to your family.

> *The winner's edge in self-dimension is to have a worthy destination and look beyond yourself for meaning in life. The greatest example of self-dimension a winner can display is the quality of earning the love and respect of other human beings. Winners create other winners without exploiting them. They know that true immortality for the human race is when a caring, sharing person helps even one other individual.*
>
> DENIS WAITLEY
> MOTIVATIONAL SPEAKER

IMPACT Story: Evan

Sometimes children have a difficult time listening to what you say to them. It would make a difference if we could listen to their actions as well as to their words. What if we saw the best in them rather than the worst? Children today are smarter than we were. They have had more exposure to the world around them than we had at the same age. Everywhere they go, they see anger, in the news, in movies, in video games. Because they live in such a fast-paced society, they are overstimulated, just as we are—and not all children are in control of their reactions.

When you tell your child to put her pajamas on and go to bed, she may not be ready. She may be overstimulated from the day's events, and may need time to relax before going to bed. You do, don't you? Reading your child a story is more important today than ever before. She needs closure with you at the end of the day. Your child needs some quiet time so she too can relax before bed. She may have had such fun being with you that she just doesn't want to go to bed yet. She's not bad if she doesn't listen; she just may not have the words to explain her feelings.

Evan's dad, Eric, played with him before bed and they had a very special time together. It had been a long time since they had had so much fun. But when Eric calmly said, "It's time to put your pajamas on and go to bed now," Evan threw his favorite stuffed animal across the room. Dad was furious. He couldn't control his reaction. His first thought was, "What kind of a child do I have? I can see him turning into an ax murderer. When he doesn't get what he wants he throws a toy across the room." Eric was furious. He lost his temper and yelled.

If he could have seen the best rather than the worst in Evan's actions, the answers may have been different. But at that moment, Eric's worst fears appeared. When Evan threw the stuffed animal across the room, Eric's brother's face flashed across his mind. He saw the jail his brother was in, and he thought, "What if Evan turns out like my brother?" Eric knew he wasn't abusive to Evan as his father had been to his brother. He was establishing simple, firm rules for Evan. But Eric couldn't quiet his negative thoughts, and at moments like these, his fears overpowered him. If he had seen Evan's actions as a sign that Evan may have had a bad day also, he may have been able to suppress his own anger long enough to discover what caused Evan's outburst.

Although the incident reminded Eric of his brother, he made a conscious decision to calm himself, as difficult as it was. He thought, "Evan is not my brother. I am not my father. I can see Evan couldn't control his impulses. My brother is like that. But Evan is good, and I know we'll find an answer. I can help him. I can respond differently than Dad. I can encourage Evan to talk about it, and help him find other ways to behave. My dad never talked. He was cruel to my brother. I turned out well because I was afraid not to listen to Dad. I don't want to treat Evan the way

Dad treated my brother. I still resent Dad. I don't want my son to have that kind of anger toward me.

"I saw my brother make the mistake of not jumping to do whatever Dad said. If he didn't stop everything at the moment Dad commanded, he was beaten. No wonder he grew up so angry. Getting into trouble with the law wasn't much different than getting into trouble with Dad. It was what my brother was used to doing. He didn't know any other way to react to Dad. I was lucky. I learned what *not to do* by watching what happened to my brother when he got in trouble. Dad used to tell my brother that he was bad. He turned out to be just what Dad said he would be. He heard it enough times. "How bad could my brother really have been? What if Dad told him he was good, and that he had made a mistake and could correct it? Would he have turned out differently?"

• • •

IMPACT in Action: Eric, Evan's Dad

I—I
"I reacted to my son the way my dad reacted to my brother. My reaction was automatic. I couldn't help it. I never wanted to yell at my son the way Dad yelled at us."

M—My
"My son deserves a better dad than I had. So did I. I don't want to be like my dad."

P—Perception
Eric's perception is that he can treat his son differently. He does not need to be like his father. "I can keep my promise to myself, and never be like Dad. I can see how I automatically repeat Dad's behavior. It doesn't feel good. I can and will be different than Dad."

A—Assumption

Eric's assumption is that his son is a good boy. "I can see him as the reverse of Dad."

Attitude

Eric can see Evan learning from the consequences of his behavior while he's young—before it's too late. "He can tell me why he threw the stuffed animal, and we can talk about a better way to handle his frustrations."

C—Communication

Once Eric understood himself, he was able to step back, relax, and help Evan look at why he threw the stuffed animal. But first he decided to tell Evan a story about how his brother acted. And he remembered to say, "I know you're not like my brother. You are a good boy. But when you threw the stuffed animal across the room without any reason, it scared me. I screamed at you like my dad screamed at me. I'm sorry. Let's talk about what happened. I think that's a much better way to behave, don't you?"

At first Evan didn't want to talk. But when he realized that Dad was interested in hearing his side of the story, Evan told him what had happened that day. He had been in a fight at school, and his teacher blamed him. His friend, Jimmy, took all of the blocks and wouldn't let Evan play. Then Evan said, "After that when Jimmy knocked over my building, I pushed him. I didn't have any other blocks to play with. He was mean. I told the teacher, but she didn't understand. She said it was my fault because I pushed Jimmy. She didn't even listen to my side of the story."

Eric said, "You must have been very angry. It didn't feel fair at all. Why didn't you tell me? Maybe I can help." Evan said, "I didn't want to go to bed tonight when you told me to. I was still angry. I don't want to go to school tomorrow. I hate my teacher."

T—Trust

Eric felt foolish. "My five-year-old isn't like my brother, and I'm not like Dad. I'm glad I took the time to calm down, sort out my thoughts, and talk to Evan. It gave me the space I needed to want to understand my son and help him with his problems. I know we'll handle it, and I'll help him do the right thing. It'll be a great start for both of us."

Then Eric said to Evan, "Thank you for telling me, son. I had a problem like that when I was five too." Evan said, "You did? What did you do?" They continued talking past Evan's bedtime but it was worth it. Dad's stories helped Evan find a way to sort out his problems. And best of all, he knew Dad understood and would help him. Evan went to bed feeling loved. He wanted to be just like Dad when he grew up.

● ● ●

Chapter 18

Principle XV.
Talking about It Is Better Than TV

When do you take the time to talk about your special feelings? When can you get your children to sit down and talk? You may answer, "Only when they have to! We're so busy with work, homework, baseball, soccer, basketball, dance class, we just don't have time." You have to eat, and drive in the car, don't you? What about before your children go to bed? Wouldn't those be good times to establish the habit of talking about the day's events—the good and bad times?

Is there importance to routine? Do you think it plays a part here? If your children were raised to sit at the table, have discussions at mealtime, and chat in the car and before bed, talking would be natural for them. What if television, radio, reading, or playing were not permitted at mealtime? Wouldn't that be a good time to discuss the day's events? If your children knew they would be included in the conversation, would that help them enjoy the discussions? They could talk about what to do in a particular situation, how to avoid a potential problem, how to avoid getting into trouble, or explain what they like or dislike. What if parents allowed their children to challenge their ideas? It might even encourage thinking and creativity.

Younger children listen and learn especially when their parents respect their comments. It makes them feel as important as the older people. How's that for building self-esteem, and self-confidence? Therefore, dinnertime, bedtime, and car rides are the most valuable opportunities for discussion and problem solving when your children are young. When conversations are part of family life, structure, security, closeness are also there.

What do you think was happening when Connie was three years old and saw Mommy crying? She just wanted to stop her. Mom's friend talked to Connie, "It's okay for Mommy to cry. She's feeling sad. She'll be better soon. She's just letting her feelings out." Connie said, "Will you love me if I cry?" She never forgot the answer, "I'll love you because you're you." It made all the difference for Connie.

Did Connie think crying was bad? Why was she afraid? When she was helped to talk about it, she said, "I just want to make sure my mommy's okay. If Mommy's not okay, what will happen to me?" Children need to have their feelings explained.

> *When everything is going badly and you are trying to make up your mind, look towards the heights. No complications there.*
>
> CHARLES DeGAULLE
> FRENCH SOLDIER AND STATESMAN (1890–1970)

IMPACT Story: Jeffrey

Jeffrey was a very unhappy child. At times he said he just didn't want to live. "I hate my life. I just want it to end." Jeffrey couldn't understand why he was so unhappy. But he was. No matter what he said, he was told that he was lying. No one ever believed him. His feelings couldn't be changed; they were his feelings.

Jeffrey felt lucky on the day he found a teacher who really cared about him. She asked him to talk after school so they could be better friends. As time passed, Jeffrey looked forward to their talks mostly because his teacher believed him. For the first time in his life, someone really listened. As they communicated, Jeffrey began to understand the source of his unhappiness and what he could do to change it. His teacher was so impressed with his ability to grasp the situation that she asked him to write a fairy tale about it.

Writing his story in fairy-tale form helped Jeffrey feel safe. If anyone found the story, it was just a fairy tale. Writing also gave Jeffrey distance from his problems. After writing about them, he was able to understand more, and to realize what he had to do to create his own happiness. No one else could do it for him. The fairy tale enabled Jeffrey to change his perception, and to finally find another way to live his life.

IMPACT in Action: The Fairy Tale

Once upon a time a family lived in a castle on the top of a mountain in Switzerland. Mom and Dad wanted their children, Jeffrey and little George, to be happy. They tried very hard to spread their love around evenly.

Jeffrey felt left out when little George was taken to the hospital. He was worried that he would never get the love he used to have before George came along. It seemed that Mom and Dad were always worried about little George. And no matter what Jeffrey did, he could never get the attention he wanted.

Jeffrey wanted to be a good big brother, but it just didn't work. The more he tried, the less it happened. Jeffrey couldn't understand why little George was so angry all of the time. He really wanted to do his very best for his little brother. But Jeffrey didn't realize that whenever he spoke to little George or played with him, his voice was mean and resentful. Little George didn't understand why Jeffrey was always mad. He wanted his big brother to be his friend more than anything in the world.

So along came a fairy godmother, and she asked George and Jeffrey both to tell their sides of the story **(Perception)**.

Jeffrey said, "I love my little brother but I don't think it's fair that Mom and Dad worry about him more than me. If George didn't complain so much, maybe Mom and Dad would have more time for me." Little George said, "I don't understand why Jeffrey never plays with me and talks to me in such a mean voice."

The fairy godmother said, "Jeffrey, you are making the **assumption** that your Mom and Dad love your brother more than you, and that's not true. It's just that each child has different needs. Your little brother didn't plan to get sick and go to the hospital, or to cry when he is sad. He is just a sensitive little boy."

To Little George, the fairy godmother said, "You're **assuming** your brother doesn't play with you because he doesn't like you, and that's not true either. Jeffrey is working twice as hard to get Mom and Dad's attention ever since you were born. He doesn't understand that he feels jealous of you but it comes out in his angry, resentful voice.

Then she spoke to both boys, "So your **assumptions are blocking your attitudes.** They block you from being happy when you are together. My advice is to **communicate** with each other about how differently you each see the world. And listen to each other. You must **trust** that you both love each other, and that you can change your attitudes. When you each hear your brother's point of view you can begin to understand how to be friends. I want you each to wish good things for your brother when you go to bed each night. When you trust that your brother will hear and feel your wishes, you will become friends.

The End.

∼ Chapter 19 ∼

Principle XVI.
Never Give Up

Mom, it is not about you. Eli is still suffering the effects of divorce. What could you say to him that proves you love him? When you tell him that he can't come to your house anymore if he misbehaves, he feels threatened and unloved. When Mom decided that Eli's happiness was more important than her feelings, things changed. By putting her feelings second, she was able to talk to her son so he felt understood. She finally realized it wasn't about her, and she came through for him by saying what she hoped would help:

> *Mom: Eli, I can imagine how difficult it must be for you to go from daddy's house to mine, and then back again.*
> *Eli: I hate it. Why did you have to divorce? You don't love me!*
> *Mom puts her emotions aside and repeats Eli's feelings to him.*
> *Mom: You wish Daddy and I were still together.*
> *Eli (hitting his mother): I hate you, I hate you.*
> *This time Mom is able to be there for him.*
> *Mom: Eli, I want you to express your feelings about the divorce and me. It's okay for you to be angry. But I can't allow you to hit me. I love you too much for that.*

    Eli: What do you mean?

    Mom: If I let you hit me, you'll think that it's okay to express your feelings that way, and it isn't. I won't be helping you, and you'll think you can treat other people this way also. It only pushes me and others away from you.

    Eli: I'm sorry, Mom. I just wanted to watch the same television program Dad lets me watch. I'm kind of used to it.

    Mom (hugging him)*: I know it's hard for you to express your feelings, but they won't hurt me. I want to do what'll make you happy. Next time, would you please try telling me?*

    Eli: I'll try. Thanks, Mom.

Dad was also aware of Eli's unhappiness, and his inability to accept the way things were. After being totally frustrated with the situation, he thought of something that might help. He decided to play a game that he hoped would help Eli feel better about what he couldn't change—the divorce.

First, Eli and Dad talked about the bad of the divorce, and then the good of it. When they said something happy, they jumped up and down and shouted, "No more yelling, yeah. No more fighting, yeah." When they said something sad like "divorce," they shouted, "Boo." They said it faster and faster until they broke out in laughter, and after a while positive feelings began to replace negative ones.

The happy aspects they discovered included how much more sensitive and understanding Eli was becoming, how much more grown up he was now, no more yelling, no more crying in bed during Mom and Dad's fights, more presents, celebrating holidays twice, celebrating birthdays twice. The sad aspects were the divorce itself, separate homes, missing each other, wanting to see Mommy and Daddy every day, lots of tears.

The divorce didn't seem so bad after that, and Eli learned to extract some good out of the bad. He learned to see the glass as half-full rather than as half-empty. Eli said, "Shouting yeah for the good things made me feel better. I still have two parents who love me a lot."

Dad's persistence paid off. He tried another approach. This one worked. Dad's motto was, Never give up, no matter how hard it gets. How lucky was Eli that his father never gave up?

Let your children see you try to fix things or solve a problem and fail. Let them see you ask for help, take a break, and come back with a new approach. When they need help, they'll come to you right away because they won't have seen you give up. So why should they?

Raising Positive Children

Raising positive children is a promise for success and happiness. It ensures that we can almost always find good in the bad things that happen to us. It's a way of approaching life that fosters happiness. We cannot prevent bad things from occurring, but if we believe that we'll be stronger and better people by overcoming these misfortunes, then we will profit from the lessons they teach us. How did your parents view the world? What did their actions teach you when you saw bad things happening to them?

Devastating events can happen. Your child may have been born physically or mentally challenged or ill. You didn't ask for it, but your life can become deeper, more purposeful, and more meaningful because of it. You will learn to appreciate the little things that others would never understand. If you can focus on the lessons, and believe that somewhere there's a reason for them, then you will focus on how to create opportunities out of challenges.

IMPACT Story: Brenda

Brenda's son was always in trouble at school. Each time the school principal called, her heart skipped a beat. She kept telling her husband, Bob, "You don't know what I go through. I break out in a cold sweat, my face is flushed, my heart is beating so loud I can barely hear what the principal is saying." Bob doesn't get it. He says, "He wasn't so bad. All boys get into fights. He'll be okay. Don't be so overinvolved."

Brenda and Bob each had a brother who was usually in trouble with the law. Why were their attitudes so different? It's an interesting question, and one that is not as difficult to answer as you may imagine. Falling in love and marrying is an unconscious, as well as a conscious, process. Nature gives us a way to work through our childhood wounds by providing a partner who usually has the same wound, but handles it in the opposite way. This was certainly the case with Brenda and Bob.

Brenda, the oldest of six children, was responsible for her younger brothers while her mother worked. Although Brenda said she didn't mind helping her mother after school each day, she acknowledged the job was overwhelming. Three of her brothers behaved, but the youngest presented an incredible challenge. He was always in trouble, and he wouldn't listen to anything she said.

Brenda remembered that time of her life with tremendous anxiety; even when her brother became an adult, she continued to worry about him. She had good reason—he was caught stealing, didn't work, and always asked her parents for money. Brenda blamed herself for his behavior. "If I had done a better job, he wouldn't have turned out this way." Even though Brenda was just a child when she took care of her brother, and she knew that as a child she wasn't equipped to raise another child, she couldn't stop blaming herself.

The birth of her son was traumatic for Brenda. She avoided him as much as she could, and hoped her husband would handle him. She didn't realize why she behaved the way she did, and couldn't stop herself. Her son was a threat to her. He caused her constant anxiety. As he grew older, his behavior was similar to her brother's, and she was angry toward him most of the time.

● ● ●

IMPACT in Action: Brenda

I—I
"I don't count. My brother counts more than me."

M—My
"I was always angry at my brother. No matter how hard I worked to take care of him, my parents gave him more attention than me. I never had my turn with them."

P—Perception
Brenda perceived that she was unable to handle her son. "I was afraid of his every outburst, and didn't know why."

A—Assumption
She assumed that he would turn out to be just like her brother. "When my son had his first temper tantrum, and wouldn't listen to me, I knew he would turn out just like my brother. I was afraid of him just like I was afraid of my brother, and I also thought my husband loved my son more than me."

Attitude
When Brenda began to look at the differences between the way her mother raised her, and how she and her husband were raising their son, she began to feel a little bit better. "When I convinced myself that we were much different than my parents, my relationship with my son changed. I realized that I was pushing my husband away from me and toward my son when I wouldn't do my share of raising him. I was turning him into my parents, and I hadn't even noticed."

C—Communication

Brenda had to communicate her feelings to her husband, to talk about how difficult her brother was, and how scared she was that their son would turn out the same way. "Then we began to plan some parenting strategies to help both of us guide our son toward listening, and doing what he was told."

T—Trust

Brenda trusted that they would turn their son around. She gave herself two new empowering messages to help her change her assumption that her son would turn out like her brother, and her attitude that she couldn't have any effect on him.

1. "My son is not my brother! My son is not my brother! My son is not my brother!"
2. "I will not give up on my son, and I will also not allow him get away with his inexcusable behavior. My mother allowed my brother to get away with it because of the guilt she felt from not being home to raise him."

● ● ●

Brenda promised herself she would follow through. She kept the memory of her brother on her right shoulder to remind her of what could happen if she didn't follow through. She also told her son, "I love you too much to allow you to pick fights on the playground and bully other children. I love you and will always be behind you. But I will not allow you to give up on yourself. You are too special." Then she would visualize her son as he could be with their guidance and perseverance.

When Brenda failed to follow through, she just visualized her brother, and that image put her right back on track. Her husband, Bob, came from a family where it was acceptable for his two sisters and six brothers to get into trouble. Brenda told him that they could do it differently. She didn't give up until she heard Bob admit, "I didn't think I could do anything to help our son improve his behavior, but after seeing what you're doing, I am ready to pitch in. I know that together we can make a difference."

Brenda and Bob realized that they didn't have to accept behavior that their families had said was "normal." They knew it would be a constant struggle to follow through, so they planned ways to check on follow-through behaviors. Brenda said, "Instead of allowing our marriage to be destroyed by our son's behavior, we found a way to strengthen our bonds to each other. In the process, we began to heal each other's childhood wounds of shame and our inability to react."

Chapter 20

Principle XVII.
Go the Extra Mile

Teach yourself and your children to go the extra mile. Make a game out of doing more than is asked of you. If your partner needs help carrying in the groceries, have the children come with you. Let them help..

When your child asks you to help her write a story, set aside time to calmly discuss what she wants to write about. Go the extra mile by allowing yourself twice the time you think it will take to help her so you won't feel rushed or impatient. If she asks you to write it for her, tell her you know she can do it, but you'll help her if she has questions, or if she wants to discuss what she wants to say.

When you take the time to explain your feelings, you are also going the extra mile, because you care enough about your child to let him know why you are upset. If you do not express yourself, you will become more upset. It is not healthy. If you carry around built-up anxiety, it will begin to show in your tone of voice, the way you look at your child, and in the way you respond to him.

Remember, your child will model your behavior. She will learn either to express her feelings by seeing you express yours, or not to express her feelings because she has never heard you express yours.

Going the extra mile also means giving your child the benefit of the doubt instead of getting angry. Try asking calmly, "Why did you say (or do) that? Something must really be bothering you, because it is not like you to behave that way. Let's figure out what it is, so we can forgive each other and start again."

Going the extra mile means *never* going to bed angry, or sending your child to bed angry. Take time to discuss what happened, and make a plan to forgive each other, so bedtime begins with a hug, and the day ends with good feelings.

Going the extra mile means tuning into your own wishes and needs, as well as your child's, and giving of yourself in the process. Paradoxically, the more nurturing you are to your child, the less nurturing he will need from you because what he gets will be sufficient.

Help Your Children Help Themselves

Your children need to know that you will help them as long as they help themselves. Make this a rule in your family. There will be many things your children will be afraid of. With a little creativity, you can help allay their fears.

Many parents don't know how to support their children during certain developmental stages. Which family went the extra mile when it came to monsters?

Serena was terrified. "Mom, Dad, help, there's a monster in here. I saw him. I really did." Her mom answered, "There's no monster, Serena. Go to bed." But Serena was scared, and no one believed her. "I don't want to stay in here alone." Her mother read her a story and put her to bed. Serena hid under the pillows and cried, but the monster didn't go away. From that time on Mom left the light on in Serena's room, and the monster didn't come.

Serena is twenty-five now, and doesn't think about monsters, but her fear of the dark has resurfaced in other ways. She still sleeps with the light on (in the hallway), and she's always with her friends. She admits she's afraid to be alone, but doesn't know why. What would have happened if her parents had believed her? Would she have fewer fears now?

Her friend Tyrone also saw a monster in his room. His mom believed him. "Where is he? I'll get him." Tyrone pointed to the closet. Mom took a broom and shooed the monster away. Ty slept well that night, but the monster came back again. So his mother said, "I think the problem is getting bigger. There's a special store that makes monster spray. It's very expensive, but I know how important it is for you, so I'll put an order in, and have it sent special delivery."

Tyrone couldn't wait. "Now I'll be in charge of my own room." He felt calmer because his mother believed him. He thought, "Mom knows I'm telling the truth, even when we can't see the monsters." The monsters bothered him less. When he ran out of monster spray, his mom reordered it until Ty just didn't need it anymore. He moved on to another developmental stage and another issue.

Ty's monster spray helped him not to be afraid of the dark. His memory of those fears changed, as new memories replaced the old scary ones. The monster spray helped him fight his fear. As an adult, he isn't afraid of the dark or of being alone.

• • •

Monster Spray

Here's the formula for monster spray, just in case you need it: Remove the label from a clear plastic spray bottle. Fill the bottle with food coloring and water. Put a new label on saying, "Monster spray made especially for ———." Then draw a picture of the monster and paste it on the bottle, so your child will know it is his or her monster spray bottle.

• • •

What would you attempt to do if you knew you could not fail?

DR. ROBERT SCHULLER
AMERICAN PROTESTANT MINISTER
CRYSTAL CATHEDRAL

Chapter 21

Principle XVIII.
One Thing at a Time, and That Done Well

There are so many things to do that it is easy to become overwhelmed. Learning and practicing the motto, One thing at a time, and that done well, makes life much simpler. Whenever your problem or your child's seems overwhelming or unsolvable do two things: (1) give yourself and your children permission to tackle the problem tomorrow, and (2) have faith in yourself. Your child will probably scream, "But my math has to be done tonight. I can't go to school without it or I'll miss recess, or flunk, or get scolded!" Whatever the reason, wait for the next day even if it means getting up very early to do the work.

Caution: Don't say, "I told you to get started earlier." Your child is already learning that lesson. Do you remember being told "I told you so"? Being patient and helping will bring more rewards, even if it takes a few tries to develop better work habits.

Tackle the Problem Tomorrow

When you give yourself and your children permission to do it another day, you are demonstrating how to ease some of the stress of daily living. Realizing that gives you space to adjust to

155

what needs to be done, and time for your subconscious to come up with another solution. Did you ever hear the expression, Sleep on it? Isn't it true that whatever happens to you looks different in the morning? Do you really want to be filled with anxiety each time you think something needs to be done "now"? Isn't it healthier for you and your children to realize that you can learn to do things at your own pace, and still make deadlines?

Knowing that you don't have to do everything right away will help you and your children plan so that most things will go more smoothly. When those unexpected deadlines just can't be helped, your body will be able to tolerate them better, because it hasn't been stressed all along.

You can also help yourself and your children by learning the most important words you'll ever say, "I can." When you know you can, self-esteem and confidence become automatic. Help yourselves accomplish as many small tasks as possible. With that experience, the larger goals will be easier to achieve.

Help Your Child Be Successful

We teach through modeling.

> *Josh: Dad, will you help me build a car with my blocks?*
> *Dad: Sure, what kind of car do you want to build?*

Josh began building the car. All he really wanted was for his father to watch him do it. Allow your children to show you the kind of help they want. Often they're not asking you to do it for them; they just want your support.

> *Dad: That looks pretty good, Josh.*
> *Josh: Gee, thanks, Dad. Do you think I should put a yellow brick on or a red one?*
> *Dad: What do you want to do?*
> *Josh: I like red.*

Dad: That's a great idea. I like the way it looks.
Josh: You do?
Dad: Yes, you really do know how to build cars.

It doesn't matter if the car doesn't turn out the way Dad would build it. It's not Dad's car. Of course Dad could do a better job, but how would that help Josh's confidence? When he asks for help, give it.

Josh: Dad, would you help me put this part here? I'm having a hard time with it.
Dad: Sure, son. Let's see how it goes. I got it, but you're right, it wasn't easy. or May I help you put this part on? It looks as if you could use an extra hand.
Josh: No thanks, Dad, I can do it.
Dad: Okay, I think you can too. But if you need me, I'm here.

By being there for Josh and helping him to be successful in one thing at a time, Josh's father is helping his son to bring that confidence into other areas as well.

Maria Montessori developed an incredible style of teaching that focused on self-reliance and confidence. Her motto was, Never do for a child what the child can do for himself. Help your children help themselves. Ask them how you can help them, and do what is asked, no more and no less. Give them suggestions, but accept their answers. If you tell them what to do, they won't want your help; when you support their efforts, they'll ask your advice and appreciate it. If your suggestions take them on a path other than what they're asking, they'll politely follow their own ideas, and that's okay—it's their project, not yours. Be there for them in the same way you would like people to be there for you.

Teach your children that they can have what they want, if they strive for one thing at a time, and follow the seven magic words: *Work hard, follow through, never give up.* Let them see this behavior in you, and show them how to experience it through the many little things that happen each day.

Some men see things as they are and say why? I dream things that never were and say 'Why not?'
ROBERT F. KENNEDY
AMERICAN POLITICIAN

Finding the Right Words

When you become conscious of how important your words are and how much they impact, positively or negatively, your child's life, you will choose your words more carefully. There may be several ideas you think would help your children. But only speak about one thing at a time so your child will absorb your message. When you know your child has taken it in, breathe deeply, and wait awhile until you approach the next topic. Remember, one thing at a time, and that done well. Imagine the impact of making one change at a time, one week at a time. At the end of the year, you will have helped quite a bit.

When you weren't aware, you could have yelled, screamed, or said anything that was on your mind at the time. Now that you have done a good job raising your children to respect themselves, they will tell you, as they grow older, when you are not respecting them. They will also tell you when you are invading their boundaries, and will let you know when you are wrong, when you are not helping, or when you have gone too far. Yet isn't this the way you would want your children to be as adults?

It may be a constant challenge to find the right words at the right place and time because you have raised people who will not accept less. The bright side is that they will not accept blame, criticism, name-calling, or abuse from others either (i.e., future wives, husbands, bosses, employees, in-laws, friends, or their children). Your children will have become a positive force to be reckoned with. Although it is the flip side of the coin, won't it be a relief to know that your children have strong wings, and can successfully leave the nest with the best possible advantages of maneuvering their way in this difficult and cruel world? When you can acknowledge the beauty of all this in your children as adults, you know your job has been well done. What more could a parent ask for?

IMPACT Story: Onnie

Onnie was raised in an abusive family. His mother was in constant fear of his father, of what he would say or do to her. She didn't dare express her thoughts and feelings. She just hoped her husband would not hit her, or scream at or beat the children.

Onnie grew up believing that no one would ever love him. He never felt loved in his family. He would hide from his father as he beat and abused Onnie's sister. His father never touched him. He was the perfect child, and too afraid to do anything wrong. He learned from his mother to lie so he wouldn't get into trouble. Onnie wanted to run away from that home, but he didn't have the courage to do it alone.

When Onnie met a woman who told him she loved him, and wanted to marry him, he was shocked. How could anyone love him? So, even though he didn't love her, Onnie thought he'd better marry her because he didn't think he would meet someone he could love. Love wasn't an option for Onnie, escape and freedom were.

Onnie's married life was no less a nightmare than his childhood had been. When his wife berated him for not meeting her needs, he hid from her. Onnie realized that he was passive like his mother, and that he had recreated the same threatening environment she had lived in. But he didn't know any other way to behave. Every day he hated his wife more. Since she controlled the finances, he felt as if he couldn't leave her. So he did what came naturally—he lied and cheated. He was as afraid of his wife as he had been of his father. He caved in to her demands, but stayed away from home as much as possible.

Onnie was also an alcoholic, as were his parents. The few times he saw them happy were when they were drinking. Although abuse usually followed the cocktails, Onnie didn't put it together. He grew up thinking alcohol would help him escape his problems. It did give him a temporary escape from his wife's brutality; but it wasn't good enough, and it didn't last.

Years later Onnie met a woman at an Alcoholic Anonymous meeting. When she began describing her life, it sounded a lot like his. He could relate to the lives the other attendees described as well. "No one in this room is here by chance," said the speaker. The members spoke a lot about anger, and how angry people blamed others for what happened to them. Light bulbs went off in Onnie's head. He thought, "This is the life I have led."

When Onnie asked his mother why she had stayed with his father, she answered, "I feel so sorry for him. If I leave him, he'll be so alone. Even after he has beaten me, when I am ready to leave, he either sends me flowers, or takes me out for dinner. He's so charming, and I really believe he is sorry, and that he won't be mean again. He cries and says he didn't mean it, and that he can't live without me. I feel so bad for him. So I stay. Sometimes things get better for a while, but not for long. I'm just tired. I don't have the courage to leave anymore. Who will take care of me? I can't seem to take care of myself."

Onnie is only too aware of how the cycle repeats itself. After talking to his mother, Onnie really felt disgusted, as if there were no way out: "I learned so much at those meetings. It's not just about your own life. When you are subject to violence, it makes you passive. I also learned that you have to fight to do things. Abusive people tell you that you're only thinking about yourself. They turn it around on you. It is not about you; it's about them putting their anger on to you. Your partner's angry, and somehow you think it is your fault.

"But I learned differently. I learned that I always blamed myself when Dad abused Mom. I kept thinking that if I were better Dad would stop. Now I realize it is the way angry people manipulate your feelings, and your life. How could Dad have put all of his anger onto us? And why did we think it was our fault? Mom also must have been abused as a child, and she was likely following that pattern from her childhood.

"It is wrong. How can a person do this to his family? I know now that when you are subject to violence and anger, it changes your own life. Abusiveness does bad things to people. It changes their outlook about what they can do in life. It makes them afraid."

• • •

IMPACT in Action: Onnie

I—I
"I'm not important. I'm not supposed to be happy."

M—My
" My life doesn't count. I am not worth it."

P—Perception
Onnie's perception is that he was supposed to be abused. He believed that it wasn't possible to have the courage to fight for himself. He learned to fight through lying. Onnie must change his perception. He must learn that lying makes his problems worse.

A—Assumption
Onnie is assuming that he will never find happiness. He is a person, and deserves happiness, just like anyone else. Onnie needs to change his assumption. He is not his mother. He does not have to live his mother's life. Starting today, he needs to make a new assumption that he, too, deserves happiness and will find it.

Attitude
Onnie is afraid of everything. He said, "It's not about getting good things. How can you think about good things? It's just one more day. If only you could live one day with peace. If you could live one day without being afraid, and with courage to speak up, and to take care of yourself."

Onnie needs to change his attitude. He needs to take one day at a time, and live it—make the best of it. The next day will follow in the same way. He needs to repeat to himself, "Do it. Do it now. You can. You can. You can," until he believes it. His courage will come. With the support of his new friends who are working one day at a time, and with his new dreams, Onnie will succeed.

C—Communication

Now it is Onnie's turn to communicate, and through communication to change his life. He must believe that now is his time to heal. He needs to allow himself to enjoy the good moments, and then create more of them. Onnie's words will help him change. His friends will hear them, and they'll also encourage him.

T—Trust

Onnie needs to trust himself and to take the time to change his attitude. He must believe that he will have the courage to speak up, and learn not to abuse himself. When a person stays in an abusive situation, that person is the abuser; he abuses himself. Onnie can stop being an abuser. He is not his father. Onnie does not have to be mean to himself anymore. He can trust that good things will come his way and take the time to make himself ready to receive them.

● ● ●

Chapter 22

Principle XIX.

Stories Teach Important Lessons

Hearing stories can help your children see their behavior in a nonthreatening way through the eyes of a storyteller. When they identify with the story's characters, they listen more intently. Doesn't that happen to you when you read a book or go to the movies or to the theater?

Telling a Story

When Sam was eight, he was having lots of problems learning how to behave at school. One day he rode his bike into a crowd of children on the playground. He could have hurt them badly. So his father decided to tell Sam a story that would teach him to think before he acted. Sam needed to understand the consequences of his behavior.

> *Once upon a time there was a happy kangaroo family that lived in Australia. One day, while the five-year-old Kanga was playing, she became so excited that she suddenly leaped on her brother without looking, and landed right on his leg. When*

the ambulance took her brother to the hospital, Kanga felt awful. Now every time Kanga played, she saw her brother watching her. She knew he wanted to play too, but he couldn't because his leg was in a cast. Kanga felt ashamed. She worried that Mommy and Daddy were angry at her. She didn't mean to be bad and hurt her brother. What could she do now?

Mommy and Daddy didn't know what to do either, because they wanted Kanga to learn to be more careful, so they asked the wisest wizard in all of the land for help. What do you think he said? "Look before you leap." When Kanga practiced that, Mommy, Daddy, and her brother forgave her, and they became a happy kangaroo family again.

Telling the story helped Sam's father find out what worked with him, and helped Sam to understand the seriousness of the problem and learn to listen better. Sam secretly knew the story was about him and was able to accept the advice without feeling threatened.

● ● ●

Formula for Storytelling

Change the number of members in a family, the sex, the place. For small children, change the people to animals; for older children, change the characters to people in other countries. Finally, change the situation so it isn't too similar to what happened with your child.

● ● ●

Although storytelling is effective, *don't overdo it*. It's also a good idea to wait for your children to ask for another story. If they don't, try again later.

Refining Your Skills

Here's another example to help you refine your storytelling skills. It's worth the effort. Children love stories, and learn from them, and you will too. They make a problem understandable.

Shelly and Billy always looked forward to summer vacations at Grandpa's as a time of family fun and laughter. But this summer was different. Grandpa was grouchy and yelled at them most of the time. They couldn't wait to go home. They told their mom, "Grandpa isn't the same grandpa anymore. He gets angry whenever he's around us. We hate it here."

On the ride home, Dad decided to tell the children a story to help them understand Grandpa's problem.

Once upon a time there was a bear family that lived together in the Rocky Mountains. They played, collected berries, told stories, and always had fun being with each other, until the day Grandpa Bear found a tree that had sharply flavored berries they'd never seen before.

After the family ate the delicious berries, everyone acted differently. Mama Bear became silly, and laughed and laughed. Papa Bear grew very quiet, and went into a corner all by himself. Baby Bear fell right asleep, and Big Brother Bear danced around the room, but Grandpa Bear became angry and started yelling at anybody in his way.

Because the bears had such different responses to the berries, Papa took some of the fruit to the wisest friend he had. The wise old bear nibbled a berry slowly, and then warned him—"Be very careful with these berries. They carry a disease called berryism. You will be able to tell anyone who has the disease by the way he eats the berries: If a bear cannot stop himself from eating them every day, even when he realizes that he becomes a nasty person after eating the berries, it will mean he has the disease."

And it came to pass that Grandpa Bear had gotten the disease because he would not stop eating the berries every day, even when they made him beastly, and he called the bears he loved names. At those times, the bear family remembered the wise bear's advice: "Sometimes nobody can help bears over this disease unless they want to help themselves. All you can do is pray as hard as you can until help comes. But remember, it is not your fault and you must not let any bear be hateful to you or treat you badly."

After that when Grandpa was mean and grouchy, both the big and little bears told him that it made them angry. Then they walked away, and didn't let him hurt them anymore.

Shelly and Billy thanked Dad for his story. It helped them understand that their grandfather had become an alcoholic, and they could do two things about it: they could pray for him, and they could stop blaming themselves for his anger.

Another way to help your children through storytelling is to change the facts of a fairy tale like "Goldilocks and the Three Bears" to illustrate your story. If your point is that people should talk about their problems rather than lie or steal, you might say,

"If Goldilocks had told us that she had no place to sleep, we would have given her a bed to sleep in. And if she were hungry, we would have fed her. Why do you think she couldn't tell us the truth?"

Your children's answers will tell you what they are thinking, what they are afraid of, and what stops them from telling the truth. Isn't that a wonderful way to solve other problems with them as well?

Stories teach important lessons. Learn how to make them work for you. Although the stories may hit home, they give us freedom and anonymity to try new solutions. They are particularly helpful for children.

> *Limitation has been an adventure; it has been an experience, and, most on this plane are experiencing it, greatly.*
>
> *Unfortunately, you forgot that there is something better and you made limitation a way of life!*
>
> *If you only knew that in unlimited thinking you transcend the embodiment, and all universes and planes, you would never choose to be limited again.*
>
> *If you only knew that and allowed yourself to receive and embrace all thoughts, you would have joy and peace in life beyond your grandest dreams.*
>
> RAMTHA

IMPACT Story

With a little ingenuity, you can create a story that will help your child change her perception of what is impacting her life today. An example:

Let's assume you have a five-year-old son who was a bully in school today, and was reprimanded for fighting with another child. Let's apply IMPACT to the situation.

Your first step would be to sit down with your son, and ask him what happened. Then take your time to apply IMPACT to the situation. Writing it down often helps your ideas take shape.

• • •

IMPACT in Action

I—I
"I wanted to play with the blocks first."

M—My
"It was my turn, and he wasn't letting me have it."

P—Perception
Your son's perception is that he can push or shove another child if he thinks he's right.

A—Assumption
Your child has also assumed that he can do whatever he wants and there won't be any consequences as long as he thinks he's right.

Attitude
His attitude is that he can take what he wants. He is so intent on what he wants that he is not thinking about the other person. He doesn't realize how his friend may feel about playing with him.

C—Communication
Your son needs to learn to use words to communicate his desires and to try to understand how his friend feels. Here's an example of a dialogue.

> **Parent:** I can see how you wanted to play in the block corner. And you are right. It was your turn. How did you feel about Jimmy when he wouldn't give you a turn?
> **Son:** I don't know. I don't think I like him.

Parent: Why don't you like Jimmy? He looks like a nice boy.

Son: He's always pushing other kids around. Nobody wants to be his friend.

Parent: So you don't like when other kids try to push you around, and take what they want, just because they want it. Is that right?

Son: Yes. That's right. Would you like your friend to push you around, and never give you a turn?

Parent: I can see your point, and I agree with it. Nobody likes it when someone grabs a toy, and just takes what he wants.

Son: Yes, that's right.

Parent: What do you think Jimmy should have done when you came into the block corner?

Son: All he had to do was to tell me I could have a turn. But he wouldn't let me play.

Parent: Do you think if Jimmy used his words, it would have helped you not to be so angry?

Son: Sure. Maybe he could have told me why he didn't want me to play.

Parent: That makes sense to me. Maybe Jimmy was in the middle of making a big building, and he didn't want it to fall down. Maybe he didn't know how to use his words to tell you.

Son: That's the problem. But it's hard to use words all of the time.

T—Trust

Now your son needs to trust that he can find the right words to use. Or he can ask for help.

Parent: It really is hard to use words. A person has to work on it. Sometimes you use your words. Does it help?

Son: Yesterday, I asked John to take turns with me. He did, too!

Parent: I knew you could do it. Do you think you forgot to use words also when you pushed Jimmy today?

Son: Yeah. I should have used my words. I'm sorry.

Parent: I know. You're a good boy. I know you're not the kind of person who takes things without asking. Do you think you can apologize to Jimmy?

Son: Okay, I will. But what happens if he doesn't listen?

Parent: What do you think you could do?

Son: I could tell the teacher. Maybe she'll help me.

Parent: I think she will. That's a smart idea. But if you still need help, let me know. We can figure it out together. I like helping you. You're a good boy, and you deserve my help. Let me know what happens. Okay?

Son: Sure, I'll talk to you tomorrow.

● ● ●

You changed the way your son looked at his friend Jimmy, and gave him other options for changing his own behavior. Instead of calling your son a bully or telling him he was bad, you helped him change the way he looked at the situation. You remembered how important it was to him to know you were proud of him. So you trusted he would feel the same way.

In any case, plan to follow through. Now you're confident that your son will get the message.

Part Three

~

Discipline Is from the Inside

~

Principles XX–XXVI

Chapter 23

Principle XX.

Discuss, Plan, and Build In Natural Consequences Before Behavior Breaks Down

It is much easier for children to behave when they feel loved and wanted, when they know what will be happening in their lives each day and what is expected of them. It's important that they be made aware of the consequences that will occur when a plan or behavior breaks down.

Children like to know when they'll be with their parents so they are free to play, and still feel their parents have special time for them. This is particularly true in our society where our lives are so rushed. Often both parents work, or are divorced, and children live in two different homes, or parents are simply too busy staying with the hectic pace of their lives.

Jake's mom planned to take him shopping after he did his homework, but Jake procrastinated and didn't get it done. So his mother built in natural consequences. She said, "Jake, I really want to take you shopping but we have to leave by five. If you start your homework now, there'll still be time for us to go together. If you don't, then I'll call a sitter and go by myself."

The key here is that his mother had to be willing to give up something in order to accomplish the larger goal—responsibility for homework. She knew she would have to pay for a baby-sitter if Jake didn't come through, and although it was expensive, she knew it would be worth it in the long run. When he realized there would be a consequence for his behavior, even when it inconvenienced his mother, his behavior changed, provided she followed through.

Some parents say, "But I don't want to change my plans. I want to have fun." That's understandable; but as far as discipline goes, that means short-term pain for long-term gain. If Jake's mother had given in, it would have sounded like this, "All right Jake, hurry up because we have to leave soon. But if your homework isn't finished, will you do it when we come home?" Of course he would have agreed. But what if they had come home late, and Jake had been too tired to do his homework? He would have learned that shopping was more important than homework; and he would have thought, "Wow, I didn't have to do my homework. Mom's great! I got away with it."

But as he grew older and was still not responsible for his homework, Mom would have said, "Jake, you have to do your homework if you want to get good marks. You don't follow through with anything!" Where would he have learned that? Giving your children natural consequences for their behavior is instructive; nagging, punishing, or name-calling isn't.

Do you remember being sent to your room for name-calling? Did that help you resolve your anger or find another way to approach the problem? Lisa couldn't stop herself from calling people names. (Her parents did it all of the time.) What if the consequence for name-calling was that she'd have to calm down, apologize, and then talk about what bothered her before she was allowed to watch television, play with her friend, or be taken to the movies? What if her parents took responsibility for their actions as well, and also made a commitment to calm down and discuss their anger instead? would that help Lisa feel better and behave differently? When your children experience logical consequences for their actions, they gain the ability to understand their lives and make better choices as a result. And when you discuss consequences in advance, children are more willing to listen and follow them.

To change one's life:

- *Start immediately*
- *Do it flamboyantly*
- *No exceptions*

WILLIAM JAMES
AMERICAN PHILOSOPHER AND PSYCHOLOGIST

~ **Chapter 24** ~

Principle XXI.
A Rule Is a Rule Is a Rule

Rules are like Tai Chi, the Chinese system of exercise. Don't oppose the force, join it, and in doing so you are in a position to direct where it is going. Rules can make your life, and your children's lives, flow more smoothly—as long as there are not too many.

Make Rules as a Family

Establish rules as a separate part of your relationship, and join your children in making rules that can work for them as well as for your family. Have family meetings where you discuss one rule that may help solve a problem. Focus on following the rule. Plan to follow up with weekly or biweekly meetings. Discuss what improved, what didn't work, and what needs to be changed. In the interim, if your children have difficulty obeying the rule, eliminate friction by placing the blame on the rule, not on your child; and insist that the rule be followed until the next family meeting, or until an emergency one is called. Suggest that will be time to discuss changes. Let them know they can discuss and change rules that don't work. Children respect fairness.

Initiating rules helps your children learn what is expected of them, and how to correct their own behavior. It's like watering plants: too much water kills the roots, but just enough keeps them healthy and the plants flourish. So use rules wisely and sparingly. Focus on the important ones. Too many rules can cause your children to rebel. Decide which ones are most important to you: being polite, not interrupting, going to bed on time. Focus on one rule at a time. When that is in place, you can begin working on another one. It's like laying the foundation of a house, brick by brick by brick. Simple rules will help your children understand their world and make it less confusing and a safer place to be in.

Rules helped make life in Ted's house more peaceful. Ted's parents loved him very much. When they lost their tempers and yelled at him, they felt guilty, as if they were terrible parents. "Sometimes I just can't help it. Bedtime drives me crazy," said Ted's dad. "Ted keeps getting out of bed. After eight or nine times, I just lose it and yell at him. He goes to bed crying, and I feel guilty. He certainly does wear me down, but it's no way for him to go to bed, especially when he says, 'Dad, you promised you wouldn't yell!'"

To begin the rules process, Dad decided to tell Ted a story about a dog from New Mexico who loved to be with his little puppy, but he always seemed to lose his patience just before bedtime. Although the story was similar to what was happening at home, the characters and the place were different. It allowed Ted to save face while exploring other ways to behave.

When Dad asked Ted what he thought the father dog should do, Ted answered quite casually, "Reward the puppy. That will help him learn." Dad was astounded, and asked Ted's advice on developing a list of rewards, and rules for earning them. After they decided, Dad reviewed the list by saying, "When you go to bed on time, you get one reward. When you do not, you lose the reward you were going to get and another reward that is on the list. If that doesn't work, then I'm going to tell you that I'm angry. That means I'm going to try not to yell, but if you still don't listen, I'll yell." Ted said, "Dad, I'll listen. Just promise you won't yell." This exercise helped Ted learn to follow rules for bedtime, and both he and Dad were a lot happier. Ted knew the consequences in advance, and when he broke the rule, Dad followed through with their plan (follow through is the secret ingredient that works won-ders). Ted clearly understood why his father yelled at him, and he knew what he could do to prevent it. Knowing he had to listen to his father helped Ted feel safer, and more in control of himself.

Following rules was equally as difficult at school for Clair. After all, for most of her life there hadn't been any rules at home. So when Clair began school, her "behavioral" problems went with her. It was difficult for her to suddenly have to follow rules when she never had before. It made her hate school, and it didn't help that her parents wanted to put rules in her home life too.

Her parents had to learn to be patient and to relax. Once they were aware of what they needed to do, things would work out, but not right away. It takes time to learn restraint, let go of old habits, and develop new ones. However, it is a good idea to look at the big picture.

Clair's teacher complained, "She doesn't listen at school. We don't know what to do with her. The rule is not to take equip-ment out of the gym, but Clair does. She says, 'It's part of the house we are building, and we can't finish it without the big brown blocks.' But the bottom line is she's taking equipment out of the gym and has a logical excuse for doing it."

Clair's father laughed. My wife doesn't follow rules either. We went to the art museum. They had ropes tied around a famous statue, and a big sign, Don't touch. Within five minutes the guards had come over to my wife and asked her to leave. She had taken Clair behind the ropes, and both were touching the statue. My wife said, 'Well that's how you get to really enjoy art.' Sometimes I feel I'm with two children. Now do you see why Clair doesn't follow rules in school?"

When both parents acknowledged the negative effect their lack of rules was having on their daughter, they realized how important it was for them to change their ways. The family decided to make rules in their house, follow through, and be consistent. It was a great start, but Clair would need a lot of experience to believe that her mother wasn't going to break the rules as she always did, and that her father wouldn't think it was so cute anymore.

As both parents changed, and rules were established and enforced in their home, Clair began to react. They made rules, one at a time, to give her time to adjust, and she did. When she knew change was here to stay, she began to respond at home. It wasn't long before her behavior also changed at school. Most important, her mother followed the rules and didn't think it was so funny breaking them anymore.

> *When a tough, challenging job is to be done, I look for a person who possesses an enthusiasm and optimism for life, who makes a zestful confident attack on his daily problems, one who shows courage and imagination, who pins down his buoyant spirit with careful planning and hard work, but says, this may be tough, but it can be licked.*
>
> HENRY J. KAISER
> AMERICAN INDUSTRIALIST (1882–1967)

IMPACT Story: The Smith Family

The Smith family had some very effective rules. They worked perfectly, but the results were extremely destructive. The problem was that neither Mr. nor Mrs. Smith realized the impact their rules had on their children. They weren't even conscious that they were rules, but the children knew what they were, and operated according to them.

RULE 1: WAIT UNTIL DAD COMES HOME

The children knew they had done something wrong when Mom said, "Wait until your father comes home." That meant when Dad walked in the door after work, they were going to be hit for what they had done. Sometimes they didn't even realize their mistake because their mother rarely explained. Instead they spent the rest of the afternoon trying to make up to Mom so Dad wouldn't punish them, or they would think up a good story to tell Dad to avoid punishment. Sam, the older child, felt angry at Mother for giving an unfair punishment. By the time Dad came home, he was ready to fight back. The more Sam fought back, the harder Dad hit him. It was a no-win situation, but he wouldn't give up. Over the years, Sam built up a lot of resentment and anger toward both parents. He never completely understood why he was being punished, but he realized that no matter what happened, he couldn't win. Rule 1 was doubly affected by Rule 2.

RULE 2: YOU'RE OLDER, YOU SHOULD KNOW BETTER

The boys were usually pretty good, and followed the other rules most of the time (i.e., be home before 6 P.M., be neat, clean your room, do your homework directly after school, take turns, etc.). But they were like most children and got into constant arguments with each other. Instead of helping them to understand and solve problems, Mom followed Rule l. Therefore, problems were never solved. The boys either played well together, or they argued just like any normal kids their age. If Sam tried to explain to his father what had happened, Dad applied Rule 2. The more Sam protested, the harder he was hit.

Since his older brother was usually hit first, Billy learned not to say anything. If his father hit him more than a couple of times, his mother would stop him. Billy figured that his mother wouldn't be saying "That's enough," if she hadn't told his dad to hit him in the first place. It didn't make sense, but Billy decided it was better to give in than to get as angry as Sam did. When his parents told Sam, "You're older, you should know better," that also didn't make much sense to Billy. He knew he was responsible as well, even though he was younger, because he started many of the arguments. But Billy didn't say a word. It just wasn't worth it. Sometimes Billy tried to be the peacemaker in the family. It was the only way he could calm his parents down, and help his older brother.

Not surprisingly, Sam turned into an angry, resentful adult. No one looked at how he was raised, or even noticed where the rage had begun.

• • •

IMPACT in Action: Sam

I—I
"I am not allowed to express my feelings."

M—My
"My family is not fair."

P—Perception
Sam's perception is that the world is not a fair place. "No matter what happens, I cannot win."

A—Assumption
He assumes that he has to fight for everything, and that his parents don't care about him.

Attitude
Sam's attitude is that he'll get back at his parents because they don't care about him. "They don't care about me. I'm just a pain. I'll get back at them when I'm older." The only problem was Sam suffered the consequences as well as his family.

C—Communication
No one ever helped Sam communicate. He didn't learn at home, or at school. Life wasn't fun.

T—Trust
Sam just exists. He still doesn't communicate well, and he has few close relationships. He's a pretty angry guy. Resentment and bitterness are the tools he uses to manage his life. Sam never learned how to negotiate his way in this world. Instead Sam spends his adulthood getting back at his parents, and the rest of the world as well.

• • •

~ **Chapter 25** ~

Principle XXII.
Don't Just Set Boundaries—
Have Agreed-on Boundaries

When you drive cross-country, do you use a map? Does it help?
Well, maps are for journeys, and boundaries are for you and your
children. They are like road maps that help you learn which
behavior is acceptable and which isn't. Knowing what you can or
cannot do beforehand gives you the opportunity to ask for what
you want, discuss the possibilities, exchange ideas with your
family, and compromise so that everyone feels satisfied with the
outcome.

Boundaries can replace yelling, nagging, and not listening.
They help you and your children intuitively respect and value each
other's opinions. Discussing behavior and negotiating rewards
and consequences teaches you how to gain control over your
lives. As the plant reaches for the sun, we reach for our independence. It's up to us to help ourselves and our children find independence appropriately. If we do not, our children will eventually
do whatever they wish, without having learned better ways to
make decisions and understand the consequences. We must help
them develop and learn about their world through discussion and
negotiation.

It can begin as soon as children are able to speak. When Tasha was two, Mom helped her find the toy she wanted to play with, instead of letting her cry for what seemed to be no reason. It gave Tasha a sense of independence and security, knowing her mother would help ease her frustrations, and laid the groundwork for talking about feelings as she grew older.

At six, after a disagreement about where she could ride her bike, Tasha and her mother wrote their first contract.

> **Mom:** *When you rode your bike yesterday, you went beyond the boundaries we discussed, and I told you that if this happened again you wouldn't be able to ride your bike the next day.*
>
> **Tasha:** *You didn't say that. I hate you. You didn't say I couldn't ride my bike today.*
>
> **Mom:** *How does it feel when you think I don't keep my promises?*
>
> **Tasha:** *I hate it, and I hate you.*
>
> **Mom:** *I'm sorry that you're so angry. I know you don't hate me, but that's the word you're using now for angry.*
>
> **Tasha** *(calmer): I am angry.*
>
> **Mom:** *I know you are, and I'm sorry you misunderstood me.*
>
> **Tasha:** *It's not fair.*

Instead of getting into a contest with Tasha, her mother headed it off by agreeing.

> **Mom:** *It isn't fair. Now do you know how I feel when you don't keep your word?*
>
> **Tasha:** *I hate it.*
>
> **Mom:** *I hate it too. Let's start fresh. Since you don't remember the consequences I told you about when you rode your bike yesterday, let's write them down today. That way, neither one of us will get mixed up.*

Writing a contract allowed Tasha to save face, and gave Mom the opportunity to show her how she could succeed, instead of feeling ashamed for not listening. (Tasha allowed her mother to do the writing because she was only six.)

Mom said, "Now, let's write the second part. We will say what the consequences will be if either one of us breaks the contract." After they discussed consequences, the contract said:

If I, Tasha, do not ask politely, or if I ride on the sidewalk when I am not allowed to, I may not ride my bike the next nice day. If I ask politely, and I wait patiently until you can watch me, I will have fifteen minutes extra time on my bike.

Love, Tasha

If you, Tasha, are polite, and have patience to wait for me, I will give you fifteen minutes extra time on your bike. If you do not come in at the time you are supposed to, you will lose a half hour the next time you ride your bike.

I love you, Mom

Since the mind is a specific biocomputer, it needs specific instructions and directions.

The reason most people never reach their goals is that they don't define them, learn about them, or ever seriously consider them as believable or achievable.

In other words, they set them up (to lose).

Winners can tell you where they are going, what they plan to do along the way, and who will be sharing the adventure with them.

DENIS WAITLEY
MOTIVATIONAL SPEAKER

Chapter 26

Principle XXIII.
Put Your Family Agreements in Writing

After discussing, negotiating, establishing rules, and setting boundaries, it is time to firm up discipline by having your actions speak louder than your words. Write contracts. Putting it in writing makes all the difference. You now have a standard that you and your children have promised to abide by; and when they forget, you can show it to them in black and white. Can you imagine what they might learn from keeping their word? What if they learned responsibility, commitment, follow through, congruence, and to keep their word? But remember, you have made a commitment to your child. Therefore, you are also expected to do what you said you would do; otherwise the contract is null and void. There is no other way to get out of a contract, except by looking at it and doing what you promised, or revising it when both parties agree. You should explain that to your child before you sit down and write it together. Even when your child is too young to read, she'll trust you enough to do the reading and writing. Naturally, the younger the child, the simpler the agreement should be.

Putting it in writing can help your child feel grown up and special. At first it will seem like a game or a new adventure. When it's time to follow through, however, you both will benefit because you both will develop a new respect for each other. A contract keeps everyone honest. Believe it or not, your child may have as many complaints about you as you have about him. Couldn't that be an explanation for occasional bad behavior?

A Word of Caution

Any of the methods mentioned here are good when they are not overdone. Anything used too much will lose both its value, and your child's interest. Use contracts like flavoring, to sprinkle on when needed.

Before writing the contract, talk to your children so they feel listened to and loved. Otherwise, the contract will have no value for them. (Remember the mirroring technique, page 132?) Don't just hear what your children are saying, listen to them.

We saw how Dad "mirrored" Anthony's feelings. When Dad told Anthony what he heard him say, Anthony felt understood. When Dad said, "I can see you feel that way because . . ." Anthony felt validated. When Dad said, "I can imagine how hurt you were . . ." Anthony felt loved. Although mirroring helped Anthony feel better, it was only the first step in trusting that his father really loved him and would be there when he promised. The conversation had gone well, and that was quite a start. But Anthony's anger was too deep to deal with in one conversation. A part of him didn't trust Dad to keep his word, and Dad knew it. Anthony couldn't imagine that his father's work could be more important than he was. He thought it was wrong.

Therefore, the next important step was to write a contract. That gave Anthony and his father a vehicle for repairing their trust in each other.

How to Write a Contract

Anthony's father finally said, "Let's write a contract in which we can both promise special time to each other no matter what else happens." As you may realize, planning and talking about what to write takes more time than the actual contract. It is like a painter who takes as much time preparing the walls as he does painting. If the walls aren't properly prepared, the work won't last.

● ● ●

Contract Writing

Stage 1.   Determine with your spouse, friend, or another person what the problem may be.

Stage 2.   Discuss the problem with the child; "mirror" the child's feelings.

Stage 3.   Discuss what needs to be put into the contract and the consequences if either party does not follow through.

Stage 4.   Write the actual contract. Be sure to include when, where, how often, how long the contract is in effect, and the consequences for not following through.

Stage 5.   Base the strength and validity of the contract on its built-in consequences, and your perseverance in following through.

● ● ●

Here's how the contract turned out:

I, Anthony's dad, promise to meet with him three times a week for one hour before school so we can eat breakfast together and ride bikes. If it rains, we will play a game. I promise to discuss our plans the night before, and wake Anthony up fifteen minutes before our meeting. We will meet no later than 7:00 A.M., and no earlier than 6:45 A.M.

Love, Dad

I, Anthony, promise to go to bed on time (8 P.M.).
Then I will be able to wake up one hour earlier
three mornings a week so Dad and I can be
together. I will have my snack, brush my teeth, get
dressed, and be ready for my story, one half hour
before bedtime (7:30 P.M.) so that I will go to sleep
on time.

I promise to be ready on time to go places with
Dad and Mom, and not to keep the family waiting
anymore. I promise to talk to Dad when I'm angry
instead of keeping him waiting and being fresh
to Mom.

Love, Anthony

If I, Anthony's dad, do not keep my promise to be
with him three mornings a week because of my
work, I promise to spend four hours alone with
Anthony on Saturday or Sunday morning on the
week that I miss any breakfast with him.

Love, Dad

If I, Anthony, am not ready on time to be with Dad
for breakfast after he wakes me up, I will miss
breakfast with Dad that day, and will only have
two breakfasts left that week.

If I do not talk to Dad about why I'm angry, and
keep people waiting or am nasty to Mom, I promise
to do one hour's work for Dad on Saturday, and
then to talk about it.

Love, Anthony

And finally

This contract will be in effect for one week, from _____ to _____. We will review the contract on Sunday morning between 9 and 11 A.M., and make changes if we think they are necessary. The contract will start on a week-to-week basis, and each Sunday morning we will decide if we want it to go for another week.

This contract, along with lots of discussion, and follow through helped repair and build a lasting relationship between Anthony and his father.

Here's another example of how Mom followed through with a contract for Maria. She started with discussions, and respected and listened to Maria. They made the rules together and set boundaries; then it was time to follow through with binding contracts for Maria and her mother. They decided together which behavior was acceptable and which was not. The discussions and putting it in writing made Maria and Mom both accountable for their commitments. And here's what they worked out.

I, Maria, promise to clean my room by 5 P.M. each Friday before I go to my friend's house or the movies. If I do not clean my room by 5 P.M. each Friday, I will not be able to go out that night. If I can't clean my room because of a special event on that day, I promise I will make an acceptable time with Mom to clean my room before I go out with my friends.

Love, Maria

*I, your mother, promise not to go into your room
and move things around unless you specifically ask
me to. I promise not to yell or nag you all week to
clean your room. I promise to show you that I trust
you will do what you said you would do. If I question you, and do not show trust, then you will not
have to clean your room that particular Friday. I
promise that if you cannot clean your room because
of a special event, we will discuss a mutually agree-
able time for you to do it. As long as you keep your
word, I will allow you to go out on Friday as
planned. If you do not keep your word, all arrange-
ments for Friday night will automatically be can-
celed, unless otherwise discussed.*

I love you, Mom

By the time most children reach ten, having discussions
and following boundaries are easier. When they want to go
roller-skating, bike-riding, or to a friend's house, both parent and
child should know what is expected.

Trust begins to develop between parent and child, and when
a larger issue comes up, it is negotiated more easily. One child
said, "I've been listening ever since I was little, haven't I?" Her
mom agreed, "You're right and I'm going to trust you on this. But
if things don't work out, will you listen to me the next time?" The
girl agreed easily. As children grow older and the issues grow
more complicated, the experience of talking and negotiating
boundaries, and writing contracts is invaluable in developing
trust and close communication between parent and child.

Interestingly, parents often learn about contracts and boundaries because they have a child who either doesn't listen, pushes
too much, or is disrespectful. Sooner or later the hard work pays
off. Boundaries and contracts become the parent's and the child's
best friend. When your child pushes you beyond agreed-on
boundaries, discuss it. Don't give ultimatums; give choices. "You

can invite your friend over to play as soon as your homework is finished, or you can finish your homework after dinner instead of having a friend visit. Or let's discuss one of your choices if you do not like these." Setting boundaries is giving choices. When you accompany choices with firmness, natural boundaries result, which allow your child to make educated decisions, and to experience the consequences of them. It gives your child the opportunity to exert free will. Learning how to negotiate helps your child gain control over his or her actions, and eventually over his or her life.

> *There are risks and costs to a program of action, but they are far less than the long-range risks and costs of comfortable inaction.*
>
> JOHN F. KENNEDY
> THIRTY-FIFTH U.S. PRESIDENT

Chapter 27

Principle XXIV.

Be Willing to Give Up Something to Accomplish the Larger Goal

When you give up a plan or alter it in order to make a point, your values are showing—and so is how important your children are to you. They learn by what they see you do, more than by what you say. When you demonstrate commitment, keep promises, respect your word, and follow through, your children will adopt the same values. Brian, David's new stepparent, called me one day in a state of total frustration. He "had had enough" of his seven-year-old's constant temper tantrums. "My wife doesn't know what to do. I'm convinced this child has a split personality. One day he's an angel, and the next day, he's a nightmare. We don't know what to do."

I soon learned that Brian's answer to every crisis was to send David to his room. After talking to me, Brian realized his son needed consequences that made sense to him. Being sent to his room didn't mean anything. "But," he said, "he doesn't seem to care about consequences." I explained to him that the consequences had no relation to David's behavior, so why would he care?

A few days later, Brian called again. David had locked himself in his room and said he wouldn't come out for the rest of the day. I smiled, as I thought about how clever David was.

> **Edythe:** *So he's turned your punishment around on you. Good! This is a great opportunity for you to learn. What obvious consequences could come from this? What makes sense to him? What are his plans for the day?*
>
> **Brian:** *He goes to school, swimming, and then grandma's.*
>
> **Edythe:** *Perfect. Tell him, he can decide to either stay in his room and miss school, swimming, Grandma's, and television. Or he can come out of his room and be ready for school right away.*
>
> **Brian:** *But I can't do that. I have to go to work, and so does his mother.*

Both parents needed to decide which came first. Would it be worth giving up time at work to help David realize that his temper tantrums were no longer effective, or should they give in as they always did? It was a dilemma.

> **Edythe:** *What do you usually do?*
>
> **Brian:** *I usually just grab him and throw him in the car. That works.*
>
> **Edythe:** *It does work temporarily, but does it solve the problem? First things first, if you set an example and stay with it, this behavior won't continue to recur. If you want to go through this again, throw him in the car. Because you are his stepfather he is convinced you don't love him, and this is his way of trying to get you to prove it.*
>
> **Brian:** *But how can I love him when he does things like this? If I have to stay home from work, I'll really be angry.*

> **Edythe:** *It's your decision. If you do stay home, make him feel loved, but not necessarily liked. You could say, "I'm feeling really angry about having to stay home from work, but I'll do it to show you that I love you, and I can't let you continue using this kind of behavior." Then give him the choices we discussed.*

Twenty minutes later, Brian called me again.

> **Brian:** *It really does work. He came out of his room and got ready for school. I can't believe it. I see your point, but it's hard to know what to do. Sometimes I'm in such a rage, I give in just to solve the problem. David expressed a lot of feelings. He said his mother made promises that she didn't keep, and that it's not my business. I told him that if I'm living in this house, it is my business. We have a lot to discuss later. We'll have to clarify the promises his mom made to keep him quiet. She feels so guilty over the divorce that she'll do anything to please him.*
>
> *Right now we're going to write down a list of consequences. One thing though, my stepson says he doesn't care about consequences.*
>
> **Edythe:** *Do you believe that?*
>
> **Brian:** *I used to, but maybe they weren't important to him. I can see how 'sending him to his room' doesn't make sense. Thanks.*

Things got better after that. When David saw that his mom and stepdad were willing to give up work, even though it made them angry, he stopped testing them. He was beginning to believe that he really was loved.

The consequences began to make sense also; and as Brian and David's mom kept their word, he knew he had to do the same. Brian learned that it was difficult to find consequences that fit the situation. So he and his wife took my advice and asked David for his input: "When you won't listen, and do what you're told, we will have to find a consequence. It's better that way, than making your mother and me yell. We would rather see you learn to get what you want by asking, not by screaming, or locking yourself in your room. The first thing we have to do is to establish simple rules like doing your homework directly after school before you go out to play. You have to be dressed and ready for school before you have breakfast, and no television before school. These seem to be the issues that cause the most problems in our house right now. Would you help us decide what consequences will make sense to you to help you learn?"

It took a while for David and his parents to determine the consequences, but working together on that issue was the best part of all. David felt that he was important to his stepdad if he would go to all this trouble for him, and being included in the planning made a big difference. The consequences they decided on were as follows: If David was not ready for school on time, his parents would not take him to the movies, or out to dinner that week (movies and dinner out meant a lot to him). David was allowed to watch television, only after his homework was completed—no homework, no television.

Both parents were aware that this was the beginning of establishing rules in their house, so they wanted to make it pleasant. They made a chart, and gave David ten stars each day for learning new habits, and doing what he promised. He could trade in ten stars for twenty-five cents. When he had enough money saved, they would take him to the store to buy whatever he wanted. They emphasized that he had earned the right to choose because he was becoming responsible for his behavior. Instead of being angry about the new rules, David began to develop a sense of pride.

His parents explained that the stars were to help him learn, and that when he did, he would feel proud, and that would be a reward in itself. They would keep the stars for an extra week until everyone was sure the lesson had been learned. Then he would be given stars for other rules they needed to implement as they grew together as a family. The important message was that they would work together to solve family problems, until each family member felt loved, and comfortable.

Decide what you want to achieve with your children. Then think about it. Is it to help your children feel loved, happy, and confident? If so, *then it's not about you, it's about them.* Take the time to understand your children's feelings, and you'll automatically do the right thing.

Victory belongs to the most persevering.

NAPOLEON BONAPARTE
FRENCH EMPEROR

Chapter 28

Principle XXV.
Negotiate

Parents usually do not like to negotiate. They say, "Are you kidding? You don't know my children. If I do that, they'll be negotiating everything I tell them. It will be impossible to get them to listen." Well, not quite. Let's recapitulate. First, you established that a rule is a rule. Then you set boundaries and understood that discipline is the art of discussion. You realized that you must be willing to give up something in order to accomplish the larger goal, and that you could only teach one thing at a time until it was done well. Last, but not least, you learned to respect your children and they will respect themselves. When you have used these tools, you are ready to allow your children to negotiate with you. If they can win, and get what they want—more power to them. You want them to be successful in life, don't you? Why not give them on-the-job training?

Childhood should be a time of joy and laughter, but it's also training for adulthood. All these tricks of the successful parents' trade are really courses in growing up. Children need an edge in learning how to gain control over their lives. It must be age-appropriate, of course. When Sarah was four, she made a deal to make her own sandwich for lunch by promising to clean up afterward. At seven she gained the privilege of walking to her friend's house across the street by demonstrating that she looked both ways when she crossed. At eleven she earned money baby-sitting. At fourteen, she negotiated a better curfew. Sixteen had the natural consequences of earning the privilege of driving the car. There's plenty of room for negotiating with your children, as long as they realize that each bargain demands responsibility from them in order for the next one to transpire.

Do you remember when you wanted a new bike and your parents said, "No way. We just bought you this one." You might have argued, "I rode my bike all of the time and I never liked it! I want the same one Kim and my friends have." Your mom or dad might have said, "You're spoiled, selfish, ungrateful, and inconsiderate. You never appreciate what you have." And you might have thought, "Gee, all I wanted was a new bike. I didn't mean to be such a bad person." Were you ashamed of how selfish you were? You might not have ever brought up the subject again. Did you still want the bike?

What if your parents had really "heard you," and realized how important the new bike was to you? What if they took that opportunity to teach you their work ethic? It might have sounded like this:

> *Parent: We understand how important a new bike is to you, but at the same time we don't feel justified in replacing what you already have. So let's see what else can be done.*
>
> *You: Gee. Thanks, what can we do?*
>
> *Parent: We could help you find some chores, so you could earn the money you need to buy a new bike.*
>
> *You: But, how will I ever be able to earn that kind of money? It will take forever.*
>
> *Parent: Let's think about the problem. How much does a new bike cost? How much could you get if you sold the one you have? How much would you have to earn? Let's write it all down and figure it out together.*

> *You: But, what if it still comes out to be too much money for me to earn?*
>
> *Parent: Let's take one step at a time. There are other options. We could shop around to see if we can find one on sale. You might want to wait until your birthday, or Christmas. We might be able to match what you earn. The important thing is that if you want a bike badly enough, we'll help you find a way to earn it.*
>
> *You: That's neat. But, I have to have it right away.*
>
> *Parent: Let's figure this out first. We can see how many hours you have to work, and how much you can earn. Then you can decide if you need it right away or if you can wait.*
>
> *You: Gee, that's great. Let's get to it right away.*

How would you have felt if it were handled this way? Would this have helped develop your responsibility, character, and appreciation of the work ethic, to say nothing of your self-esteem? How would you have approached the next situation that occurred? How much would this have strengthened your bond with your parents? What about the self-confidence you would have gained in learning how to develop ways of becoming the master of your fate?

We are not here just to survive and live long....

We are here to live and know life in its multi-dimensions to know life in its richness, in all its variety.

And when a man lives multidimensionally, explores all possibilities available, never shrinks back, from any challenge, goes, rushes to it, welcomes it, rises to the occasion then life becomes a flame, life blooms.

BHAGWAN SHREE RAJNEESH

Chapter 29

Principle XXVI.
Let Your Children Win the Battles, You Win the War

Look at the bigger picture, and help your children feel trusted, respected, and loved. It is okay to give in on small things. Let them win the battles—a reasonable time to go to bed, time to do homework, what clothes to wear, how they wear their hair—while you win the war helping them to be responsible for their word and their actions. Then they will grow into people you respect and love.

Why not let your children help you think of the consequences that will help them learn and follow through. The punishments they come up with will usually be much more effective than what you can give them, and the process will help them develop control and self-discipline.

Work together to make the consequences relate to their actions, so they can learn and grow from their mistakes. Often, your children may think of consequences that are much too harsh for the situation. Then it will be important for you to tone them down; overpunishing, even if children suggest it, is not helpful or necessary. It's a valuable area for discussion; it will help both of you understand how the other thinks.

Focus on what's important, and learn all that you can to be the best parent you can be. After all is said and done, the true expert is inside you. No one knows your children as you do. My hope is that this manual can become your inner guide to parenting. In looking back I realize the mistakes I made came from *not* listening to my "gut." When I followed advice that didn't feel right, it was because I thought the advice came from "the experts." If I had tuned in to my instincts, I could have tailored the advice to the needs of my children.

How many times have you said, "When I was a kid I could do that, why can't they?" Your children can do more than you think. Why not let them? It can't be said often enough: Let your children win the battles, you win the war.

As you've already found out, parenting is not easy. What if things don't go as planned? Life has a way of scrambling us up! But we can always re-evaluate, begin again, and zoom in on what really counts—love and self-worth.

Even the U.S. Constitution has "what if" provided for—that's why we have amendments. If it's good enough for 250 million Americans, it's good enough for parents.

What the hell—
You might be right,
You might be wrong...
But don't just avoid.

KATHARINE HEPBURN
AMERICAN ACTRESS

The End

You have just read the twenty-six challenges you and your children encounter on a daily basis, and illustrations of how the principles set a structure for solving them effortlessly.

1. Accept, and apply, one principle at a time for a two-week period.
2. Begin now.
3. Continue until each principle becomes a part of your life. Then begin again until every moment is a challenge and a joy to behold.

A Fairy Tale

And it came to pass that people put the Twenty-Six Principles in their kitchens, and read one each day. When they became part of their lives, parents began to write stories of their own, and added them to the principles. Each one illustrated new and better ways to teach themselves and their children.

And it was wisely stated that, "It takes groundwork of constant repetition to change your ways." So it was prophesied that when people developed the lifelong habit of assimilating this information on a daily basis, love and goodness would begin to reign, and would replace the harshness, criticisms, and negativity of our time.

And, as the principles automatically became a part of the people's waking moments, there slowly and effortlessly developed responsible, confident, caring, happy children, who became the responsible, confident, caring, happy adults everyone longed to know. And love truly began to reign. It was prophesied that humanity would change as guilt, name-calling, shame, and abuse were banished from our lives forever. As children and parents began to be more caring of themselves and each other, they were happier. Word spread quickly. And it came to pass that generations of children grew up not knowing of, nor comprehending the barbaric practices of yesteryear: name-calling, criticism, abuse, shame, and guilt. Stories were told of how it used to be in ancient times, and people were grateful for having acquired a new powerful way of living.

Index